TIGHT-SLOT FOOTBALL:
A Flexible Attack

TIGHT-SLOT FOOTBALL:
A Flexible Attack

Jack Maddox

Parker Publishing Company, Inc.
West Nyack, New York

© 1983 by

PARKER PUBLISHING COMPANY, INC.

West Nyack, N.Y.

Library of Congress Cataloging in Publication Data

Maddox, Jack
  Tight-slot football.

  Includes index.
    1. Football—Offense. 2. Football—Coaching.
I. Title.
GV951.8.M23 1983   796.332'2   82-22440
ISBN 0-13-921205-1

Printed in the United States of America

WHAT THIS OFFENSE WILL DO FOR YOU

This book describes an offense that has enjoyed considerable success without superior material. Its uniqueness lies in the placement of the slot back. Because of his location as a close back in the slot between the offensive end and tackle, he not only presents difficult problems for the defense to solve, but he can be utilized in many ways that are not available to the usual wing set. Here are some of the many advantages of the system.

- It will help you win more games because its concept, design, and flexibility offer you an offensive capability and consistency against any defense.
- This offense will be successful for teams having nothing more than the usual caliber of high school athletes.
- Favorable blocking angles, feints, and running routes place an extra burden on the defense.
- Your crucial off-tackle play will be more successful. Because of the unique placement of the slot back, the defensive tackle is always outflanked by a close blocker who has an advantageous blocking position.
- Your quick counters will hit more quickly, and more effectively, because the slot back is lined up closer to the point of attack.
- You can use the slot back as a runner, pass receiver, and multiple blocker.
- Your attack has a built-in change of pace. Plays directed at the slot side have the crunch of single wing power, and plays to the off side hit with the explosive speed and deception of the "T."

9

- You will have a balanced attack. The basic Red Series features an equal number of plays to both sides of center.

- You will get more blocking at the point of attack as you run the multiple use Blue Series.

- Using the White Series, your team will hit quickly—inside and outside—away from the set of the slot, and quick counter away from the flow.

- You will conserve practice time as you use the system of streamlined drills that are expressly designed to simulate actual game conditions.

- Finally, your players will gain confidence from game to game as the Tight-Slot attack helps them experience more and more success.

Jack Maddox

Contents

CHAPTER 5

THE MULTIPLE-USE BLUE SERIES (*cont.*)

CHAPTER 6

THE TIGHT-SLOT PASSING GAME   103

CHAPTER 7

TIGHT-SLOT PLAY-ACTION PASSING   113

CHAPTER 10
AUDIBLES FOR THE TIGHT-SLOT ATTACK (cont.)

CHAPTER 11
BASIC TIGHT-SLOT DRILLS   165

CHAPTER 12
DRILLS FOR THE RUNNING GAME   171

CHAPTER 13

DRILLS FOR THE PASSING GAME   185

1

Theory and Organization for the Tight-Slot Attack

A SOUND OFFENSIVE PHILOSOPHY

The number one objective of the offense is to score. In theory, there are more ways to score on defense, but points usually come with more frequency to the team that has the ball. There are several reasons for this.

First of all, the team that has the ball has the initiative. It has the advantage of knowing when the ball will be put in play, and where and how it will proceed. With this knowledge and with a reasonably sound attack, the offense can be expected to continue to move the ball with consistent gains. A repetition of gains will result in two more advantages—field position, and time of possession of the ball. Therefore, it is expedient to have an offense that is designed to give the team with the ball every possible help. Such an offense is the Tight-Slot.

In attacking the defensive team, there are but two basic methods of moving the ball—the run or the pass. In theory, then, the team with the ball should simultaneously threaten the run or pass on every play so that the defensive team is always confronted with a dual responsibility, and cannot concentrate exclusively on the run or on the pass in its defensive plan.

Unfortunately, in actual practice, it is very difficult to maintain both threats equally and at the same time; therefore a coach usually decides which particular scheme he will emphasize—run or pass. While he might strive for equal balance between the two, available players tend to color his decision. In addition, dominant local weather conditions can be a decisive factor.

The Tight-Slot threatens the run first and then the pass. Consequently, a very important part of the passing attack is passes that are designed as play-action passes. In other words, the initial movement has a run look, followed by the throw. This does not mean that drop-back passes are not included in the offense. They are present and used in obvious passing situations, and are complemented with screens, draws, and statues.

SET OF THE BACKFIELD

The backs are aligned to get power to the slot side and speed with deception to the off side (Figure 1-1).

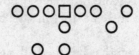

Figure 1-1
Backfield Set in the Tight-Slot

ADVANTAGES OF THE TIGHT-SLOT

In order to meet the requirements of our offense theory, it is helpful to have a set that structurally favors the team with the ball. Furthermore, the design of any particular play ought to include favorable blocking angles. The path of the ball carrier, together with various feints, should aid the blockers. Finally, the offensive set should assist in running the ball off tackle. An offense that cannot consistently run off tackle is a severely limited offense. In the Tight-Slot that chief defender—the defensive tackle—is put at a disadvantage. This is simply because, in lining up against the Tight-Slot offensive set, that tackle is always outflanked on the line of scrimmage by a close blocker who has an advantageous angle on him.

There are several other advantages. The slot back is used as a blocker, as a pass receiver, and as a runner, who in quick counters and reverses, is lined up more closely to the point of attack.

THREE BASIC SERIES

The Red Series is taught first. It features several points of attack to either side of the center, and will be described in full in Chapter 3.

Our White Series, described in Chapter 4, complements the Red Series, and features running away from the set with speed and deception.

Chapter 5 depicts our multiple-use Blue Series, which features power blocking at the hit area.

PERSONNEL REQUIREMENTS

In putting together the Tight-Slot attack, we look for players with certain characteristics to fit into the line and backfield positions. If we are successful in this, we can run the the offense effectively.

Slot End: Here we first look for a blocker with size. Most of the time he will be working against the defensive tackle. We have often converted a tackle to this position. His pass catching ability is secondary to his blocking.

Slot Tackle: We use our largest tackle at this spot. He, too, will be opposed by the defensive tackle most of the time. In addition, most of his downfield blocking will be in the close secondary. He need not have great speed.

Slot Guard: This lad must be agile and a good blocker. His pulling assignments on many plays requires him to have good speed.

Center: In this position, we like a player with good size. He need not have great speed because his blocking is usually "on," "away," or in the close secondary. Good height is desirable because it keeps the quarterback from being tied up in a crouch to receive the snap.

Off Guard: His attributes are exactly the same as those of the slot guard, but he must have greater speed. As a lead blocker, he has farther to run, and must keep ahead of the backs.

Off Tackle: Good size is helpful, but he must have greater speed than his counterpart. He often must block in the deep secondary and must be able to get there in a hurry.

Off End: We place our best receiver here. Size and height are helpful, and good speed is vital. In addition to deep secondary blocking, he is our prime passing target.

Slot Back: We look for a good athlete here. He must have enough size to block, and speed for the counters and reverses. He also needs good hands.

Fullback: We use our biggest back here. Great speed is helpful but not vital. He must be able to hit the line with authority. Many of our plays begin with an inside fake to our fullback to set up the blocking or to hold the linebackers temporarily in position. He must be able to make the defense respect his inside running threat.

Halfback: This is our best running back. Size is good, but speed and agility are essential. If he can pass, that is an important bonus.

Quarterback: Here we look for a "take charge" player. In addition, he must be agile, to execute our pivots and fakes. He must be an adequate passer. Finally, he must have enough intelligence to learn our attack, and put it into execution.

LINE SPLITS

The Tight-Slot uses a balanced line with the slot back set inside his end. Against an even defense he is one yard deep and two feet outside his tackle. The slot end is on the line of scrimmage and two feet outside the slot back. If the defense is odd, the slot back closes to within one foot of his tackle, and the slot end moves to within one foot of the slot back. Guards remain constant with a one-foot separation from the center, and the tackles are always aligned two feet from their guards. Then the off end takes a three-foot split from his tackle. The relatively close splits in our line aids us in getting to the corners more quickly, and the narrow space makes it more difficult for the defense to blitz through these close quarters (Figures 1-2, 1-3).

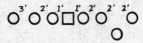

Figure 1-2
Line Splits Versus 6-2 Even Defense

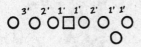

Figure 1-3
Line Splits Versus 5-2 Odd Defense

NUMBERING SYSTEM

The system of numbering holes illustrated here designates the areas of attack over the position of our own offensive linemen. This is done because it is not always known where the defensive players will align, but the location of our own linemen is well known (Figure 1-4).

The backs are numbered as in Figure 1-4. The fullback is aligned directly behind the ball, about three and one-half yards

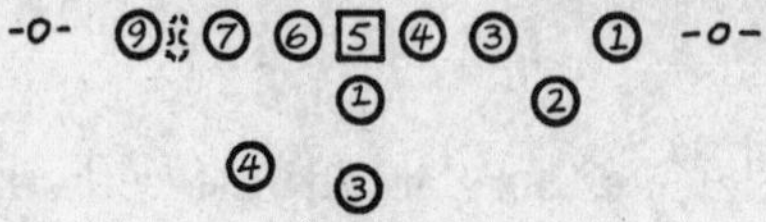

-o- ⑨☷⑦ ⑥ ⑤ ④ ③   ① -o-
              ①   ②

        ④   ③

Figure 1-4
Numbering System

deep. His exact depth will depend upon his speed. The halfback straddles the inside leg of his tackle, and aligns his toes with the heels of the fullback. The quarterback is directly behind his center, and the slot back is one yard in depth.

HUDDLE AND SIGNAL SYSTEM

We use a pool rack huddle. All players except the quarterback take their positions with heads up and hands on knees. The quarterback stands erect with his hands on his hips (Figure 1-5).

Now the quarterback is ready to give the play and starting count to the team. He does so in the following manner: (1) calls the series and play number; (2) gives the starting count; (3) calls "Center." The center leaves the huddle, rushes to the line of scrimmage, and sets over the ball as a marker for the rest of the linemen. Simultaneously, the remaining linemen and backs come erect with hands now positioned on their hips. (4) The quarterback cries "Break" and, clapping hands, the remainder of the team quickly approaches the line of scrimmage and assumes a two-point stance with their hands on their knees. At the command "Set" all players assume their regular stances, read the defense, and prepare to execute on the designated snap count. The snap signal is the word "Hit," and the ball is passed on the first, second, or third call. The

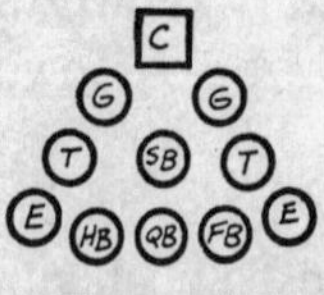

Figure 1-5
The Huddle

count is nonrhythmic. As the quarterback cries "Hit," the entire team echoes his call by calling out "Hit," and firing out on the designated call.

USE OF AUDIBLES

Although we do not feel the continuous need for the use of audibles, there are times when the defensive set is a "gift," and it is wise to accept it. Our audible system is simple but effective. It can be used in squad scrimmages as well as in games.

To audibly change the play at the line of scrimmage, our quarterback, after crying "Set," now repeats the takeoff number given in the huddle, and this alerts the team that a new play is to be called. If the snap in the huddle was given as "2" and the quarterback wishes to change the huddle play from Red 41-Square to Red 34-Trap, he would, after setting the team, call 2-34, 2-34. The team is alerted that the new play is 34-Trap, adjusts its blocking assignments, and fires out on the second "Hit"! If the quarterback had wished to fake an audible, he might have called 1-34, 1-34. This, of course, is not meaningful as the huddle snap count was 2, not 1. Consequently, the team runs the play given in the huddle.

TEAM TAKEOFF

Along with running, blocking, and tackling, we consider team takeoff a very important football fundamental. A team that wants to run the ball must fire out with a uniform, solid forward wall. If offensive linemen do not get out in unison, spaces appear along the offensive front, and the defense rushes into these spaces. Therefore, it is imperative that the team fire out as one, and serious effort is made to assure this. Every day the team fires out on the seven-man sled—complete with backfield. Coaches are stationed at each end to watch and correct. The same effort is made during signal drills; coaches are at the ends to watch for and encourage uniformity. We constantly emphasize that with sharp, vigorous, and uniform takeoff, even a play that has not been blocked well has some chance of gain.

2

Tight-Slot Terminology and Blocking System

So that blocking rules and other instructions can be more easily understood and applied, a glossary of key words is furnished to the staff and team. This usage, common to all, promotes a clearer understanding of what we are teaching. Like all teaching, it is not what the instructor knows but what the pupil knows that counts. And, we do everything we can to give the squad members assistance in learning.

GLOSSARY OF TERMS

Alternate Blocking: A switch in the blocking scheme at the point of attack.

Audible: A method of changing the play called in the huddle after the team has taken its position on the line of scrimmage.

Away: Blocking away from the side of the play call.

Backer: The defensive linebacker closest to you and the play side.

Corner: Pull out of the line and block out (or in) on the first defensive player who shows on, or beyond, your own end.

Entertain: The pulling lineman acts against the defender at the corner. The offensive player fakes a high inside shoulder block, screens that defender's vision, slips inside, and then blocks downfield.

Even Defense: The defense is even when there is no defender on the line of scrimmage opposite our center.

Fill: The closing off of the area to his inside that has been vacated by a pulling lineman.

Lane: The downfield extension of the hit area. Also, a blocking rule in which a player sprints to the "lane" and there blocks the first defender he sees.

Monster: The second defensive player lined up outside our end when the defensive team is set in a 4 deep.

Odd Defense: The defense is aligned in an odd alignment when an opponent on the line of scrimmage is directly opposite your center.

Off Side: That side of our offense team that is aligned next to our center on the side away from the slot back.

On: An opponent is deemed to be on you if he is aligned on your outside shoulder to the outside shoulder of your teammate inside you.

Slot Side: The side to which the slot back lines up.

Stack: The position of two defensive players in which one is placed in a gap in the line of scrimmage with a teammate directly behind him.

Tandem: The positions of two defensive players in which one is placed head on an offensive lineman and a teammate is directly behind him.

Trapper: An offensive lineman who pulls close behind his own line and blocks an opponent who has been let in.

WHY BLOCKING RULES?

Because of the number and variations in modern defenses, some clear and concise method of dealing with this diversity is a necessity. Consequently, brief, descriptive word images are used to convey to each player exactly what he must do with respect to any given play. When an offensive blocker knows without question what he is to do, he can do that with confidence.

APPLICATION OF RULES

Our offensive linemen on the slot-back side of our formation are known as: S.E. (Slot End), S.T. (Slot Tackle), and S.G. (Slot Guard). Our Center is C. On the side away from the slot back are the O.G. (Off Guard), O.T. (Off Tackle), and O.E. (Off End). Illustrated below is play Red 41-Square with its base blocking rules and their application by the offensive linemen (Figures 2-1, 2-2).

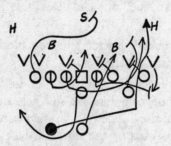

Figure 2-1
Red 41-Square Versus 6-2 Defense

BASE BLOCKING RULES

        S.E. Inside
        S.B. Backer
        S.T. On; inside

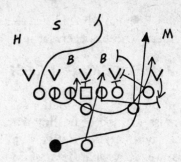

Figure 2-2
Red 41-Square Versus 5-2 Defense

S.G. Corner
C. On; away
O.G. Lead
O.T. Fill
O.E. Lane

APPLICATION OF BLOCKING RULES

S.E. Applies his "inside" rule and blocks the first defender to his inside.

S.B. Uses his "backer" instructions and blocks the linebacker closest to him and the play.

S.T. His instructions are "on; inside." In the 6-2 defense he has no defender opposite him and so blocks the first defender to his inside. In the 5-2 defense he is opposed by a defender on him, and, assisted by the slot end, blocks that defender.

S.G. "Corner" is his rule. Accordingly, he pulls close behind his own line and blocks out on the first defender showing on or beyond his own end.

C. His rule is "on; away." Because there is no player on him in the 6-2 defense, he blocks the first opponent away from the play side. In the 5-2 defense, he blocks the defender opposite him.

O.G. Applies his "lead" rule by pulling behind his own line, turning up through the hole area, and leading the ball carrier upfield.

O.T. His rule is "fill." In the 6-2 defense he pulls around the center's block and fills the vacated area. Against the 5-2 defense, he fills the area vacated by his guard and protects against a blitz by the close backer.

O.E. Applying his "lane" rule, the off end sprints to the lane area and blocks the first defender he sees.

Each player, in addition to his blocking rules, is furnished with a question-and-answer sheet concerning those rules. This has been a successful method of teaching team offense without cluttering minds with lengthy descriptions of techniques and dos and don'ts. Blocking assignments are rehearsed over and over again until defensive recognition and then execution becomes automatic. As that plateau is reached, the techniques and execution will improve; the blocker is now able to concentrate on the block itself.

QUESTIONS AND ANSWERS

Q. Why do we use blocking rules?

A. Blocking rules tell us whom to block. No one can block effectively without knowing which opponent to hit.

Q. I am a "lane" or "lead" blocker. Should I pass by a member of the defensive team who may be able to get in the running lane in order to block a defender farther downfield who is already in the lane?

A. No! Never pass up one defender to get to another.

Q. Is it possible for a defensive player to be "on" me and also a backer?

A. No! Backers are always off the line of scrimmage.

Q. I am a 3 tackle, and a 41-Square has been called. When I get to the line of scrimmage, I find a defensive player in both my inside and outside gaps. What shall I do?

A. Block the man in the inside gap; he is, by definition, "on."

Q. I am the slot end in the same situation. What will I do?

A. Block the man in the inside gap for the same reason.

Q. I am the ball carrier and see the same situation. What shall I do?

A. Veer outside over the block of the slot end.

Q. I am the "trapper." When I get to the hole area there is no opponent there. How shall I react?

A. Turn up into the running lane and block the first defender you see.

Q. I am a "corner" blocker. When I arrive at the corner there is no one there. What now?

A. You are really a long trapper. Turn up into the running lane and block the first defender you see.

Q. I am the slot back and my assignment on a "O" call is to turn the defender in. When I arrive there I find he has crossed deep or is retreating to the sideline. What will I do?

A. Drive him out. The ball carrier will cut up inside your block.

Q. I am the "lead" blocker on a "1" call. When do I turn upfield?

A. As soon as you get there. It is important to get upfield as soon as possible.

Q. I am a 7 tackle and cannot get to the backer soon enough. What do I do?

A. If all else fails, clip him from behind. You are in the area of close line play and it is perfectly legal.

Q. What is the best type of downfield block to use?

A. A running shoulder block. Our back will use you as a dodging post. The important thing is to keep contact with the defender.

Q. Is there really any difference between an off-tackle play and an end run by our team?

A. Occasionally there is little difference. It really depends upon the play of the corner defender. If he is coming in tight, we will turn him in (or knock him down) and the ball carrier will bend outside. If the defender is boxing or playing loose, we will drive him out and the runner will make an inside cut.

Q. I am an off end and my assignment is often "lane." On corner plays away from me, I have difficulty in getting into the lane soon enough. How can I correct this?

A. Get off faster and sprint a course closer to the line of scrimmage. DESIRE is often the key to that problem.

Q. I am a slot guard and my assignment is "corner." How do I get the job done?

A. Normally you will block out on the first defender on, or beyond, your slot end. However, if that defender is crashing, knock him down or turn him in, and the runner will cut off your block. You have the option of taking the defender out or in.

The use of this distributed question-and-answer sheet has been of great value in teaching our defense to the squad.

HOW WE LOOK AT DEFENSES

The Tight-Slot is not interested in the *names* of defenses. Because we are primarily concerned with beating a crucial part of the defense—and not all of it—defensive names have no real use. What we are vitally interested in is the placement of the defensive players at the point of attack. Because of our use of blocking rules we are able to get optimum blocking at that point. In passing situations, we are primarily interested in seeing whether the deep secondary is 3 or 4 deep.

Because there are almost unlimited combinations and linebacker arrangements, later diagrams and explanations will show and explain how we handle slants, stacks, tandems, blitzes, etc.

Once again, our primary objective is to get the best blocks in the hit area.

3

The Basic Red Series
in the Tight-Slot

THE BASIC SERIES

The Red Series is the basic, hard core in the Tight-Slot attack. It features three plays to either side of the center, and in itself, is almost a complete running offense. It is the first taught, and is used a good percentage of the time in games.

In this series the quarterback has three optional moves that increase the flexibility of the series and pose different problems to the defense (Figures 3-1, 3-2, 3-3).

The Roll option poses the threat of a quarterback keeper or bootleg pass, and has a tendency to slow the defensive secondary rotation. When the quarterback uses the Drop action, he is defi-

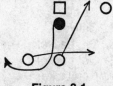

Figure 3-1
Roll

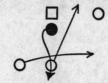

**Figure 3-2
Drop**

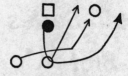

**Figure 3-3
Chase**

nitely threatening the pass, and when the Chase maneuver is employed, the defensive flank is confronted with both an inside and outside run, and the secondary with a pass. These three variations by the quarterback increase the problems of the defense all out of proportion to its simplicity for the offense.

RED 33–DRIVE

The 33-X is the base play in the Red Series. This inside buck sets up all but two of the remaining plays in the series, and its execution is vital to the rest of the Red attack (Figures 3-4, 3-5, 3-6, 3-7).

BASE BLOCKING RULES

S.E. Inside deep defender
S.B. Side deep defender
S.T. Inside
S.G. Outside
  C. On; backer
O.G. On; backer
O.T. Fill; backer
O.E. Side deep defender

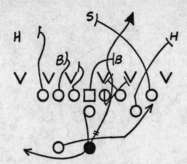

Figure 3-4
Red 33-X Versus 6-2 Defense

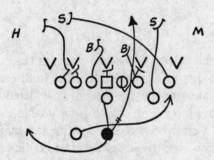

Figure 3-5
Red 33-X Versus 5-2 Defense

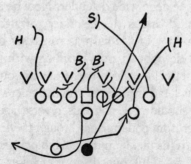

Figure 3-6
Red 33-X Versus 4-4 or Split-6 Defense

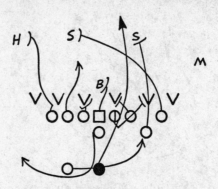

Figure 3-7
Red 33-X Versus 4-3 or 6-1 Defense

Position Play

The slot end drives off the line and sprints for the deep inside defender. He wants to keep that defender from entering the running lane. He aims at the numbers of that defender's jersey and applies a running shoulder block. If he is unable to use a shoulder block, he uses a cross-body block. In this, the target is the opponent's mid-section, and the slot end throws his closest hip there and extends his leg on that side to build a barricade between the defender and the runner.

Jab-stepping to allow the end to clear, the slot back sprints to a position inside the deep wide defender. Now he applies a running shoulder block, and drives the defender toward the sideline. If necessary, he too, may bridge with a cross-body block.

The slot tackle, who is cross blocking with his guard, blocks the first opponent inside. He drives from his outside leg, makes certain he gets his head in front of the defender's crotch, and hits with his outside shoulder. Using this reverse shoulder block, he keeps the defender from penetrating through the line of scrimmage.

Working with his tackle in the cross block technique, the slot guard drop steps with his outside foot, crosses behind his own tackle, and uses his outside shoulder to drive the defender out.

The center, if covered, uses his near shoulder to drive his

opponent away from the hit area. He continues to work around that opponent to keep him from rolling back into the running lane. If uncovered, the center uses a running shoulder block to drive the closest backer away from the path of the ball carrier.

If covered, the off guard uses his outside shoulder to keep his opponent from the run area. He continues to work around that defender to prevent his releasing into the area of the ball carrier. If uncovered, the off guard blocks the closest backer. He releases on a course that will take him beyond the backer so that he can block him back towards the line of scrimmage.

The off tackle's assignment is "fill; backer." He must prevent any opponent from crossing the scrimmage line in front of him.

Before making his approach to the deep outside defender, the off end "influence blocks" the first opponent inside on the line of scrimmage. He steps at that player with his inside foot and delivers a slam with his forearm on the same side. He makes him conscious of outside pressure—and then releases. On this, the off end is setting up that defender for the time when the off end will be actually blocking on him—not releasing.

The quarterback reverse pivots to the slot side. Holding the ball close to his stomach in both hands, he retreats straight back. He slips the ball into the pocket formed by the running back with the hand closest to the line of scrimmage, and then continues to fake a roll, drop, or chase.

Watching the hole area, the fullback forms a pocket by placing his outside arm and hand, palm up, across his midsection at belt level. His inside arm and hand, palm down, is held across his chest and parallel to the ground. Upon feeling the ball, he clamps it with both hands and forearms and drives into the hole. He must not look at the quarterback, but concentrates on the in-line blocking, and the blocks on the linebackers. He is then looking for the area being opened by the deep downfield blockers.

The halfback comes straight across to fake a take from the quarterback who is continuing straight back to intersect his path. He, too, forms a pocket, fakes a reception by clamping his arms and hands, dips his inside shoulder, and drives into the off-tackle area.

Coaching Points

In reversing out, the quarterback takes a short step back with his outside foot, pivots on that foot, and, with his back to the line, drops straight away to intersect the path of the halfback. It is his responsibility to place the ball correctly in the pocket formed by the ball carrier. He must then fake the ball to the halfback before his roll, drop, or chase actions. The quarterback's faking, if convincing, will slow the defensive reaction, and so enhance the success of the play.

RED 41-SQUARE

Red 41-Square is designed to break inside the defensive perimeter between the defending tackle and end. After the success of 33-X, the opposing tackle and linebacker are now concentrating on stopping that play, and this allows us to get good blocks on both those defenders. With a block out on the opposing end, and a lead blocker for our runner, we are in position for consistent gain (Figures 3-8, 3-9, 3-10, 3-11).

BASE BLOCKING RULES

S.E. Inside
S.B. Backer
S.T. On; inside

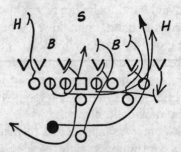

Figure 3-8
Red 41-Square Versus 6-2 Defense

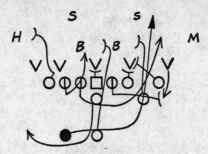

Figure 3-9
Red 41-Square Versus 5-2 Defense

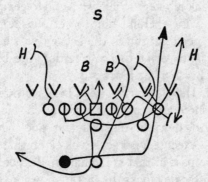

Figure 3-10
Red 41-Square Versus 4-4 or Split-6 Defense

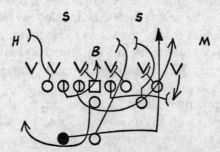

Figure 3-11
Red 41-Square Versus 4-3 or 6-1 Defense

S.G. Corner
 C. On; away
O.G. Lead
O.T. Fill
O.E. Side deep defender

Position Play

The slot end blocks the first defender inside. He must get his head across that defender and hit with his outside shoulder. To make sure of this, he aims his head across the crotch of that defender. The slot end must not allow any penetration.

The slot back jab steps to allow his end to get across in front of him, and then swings behind him to get outside position on the line-backer. He need not run to the backer but simply sets up in a position so that, to get at the ball carrier, the backer must run through him. This is a key block.

If covered, the slot tackle steps into his opponent with his inside foot and shoulder to prevent penetration. He knows that the slot end is blocking down on that defender, and that the slot tackle and slot end will execute a post-drive block on that opponent. The slot tackle is the post in that combination. If there is no defender on him, the slot tackle blocks the first man inside. He must get his head across that defender's crotch, prevent penetration, and drive him down the line of scrimmage.

Pulling close to the line of scrimmage, the slot guard gets an inside angle on the end defender, and, using his outside shoulder, drives the defender toward the sideline. However, if that defender is coming in hard and tight, the slot guard will knock him down with a chop or cross-body block, and the ball carrier will adjust his cut to the outside.

If an opponent is playing opposite him on the line of scrimmage, the center uses his close shoulder to block him, and continues to work around him to keep the defender from rolling off into a good pursuit lane. The center is not using a drive block to move the defender; he is simply keeping him out of the pursuit.

The off guard, who is the "lead" blocker, pulls laterally and deep enough so that he can keep ahead of the ball carrier while running an arc that will let him enter the hit area with his shoulders parallel to the line of scrimmage. In that position, he is able to adjust quickly to the moves in the defensive secondary. His job is to block the first defender he sees who is a threat to the running lane. He will drive at that defender with a running shoulder block, maintain contact, and let the ball carrier use him as a dodging post.

The off tackle fills the area vacated by the pulling-off guard. If there is an opponent over that guard, the off tackle pulls around his center and fills that area as the center is blocking on that defender over the off guard. If there is no opponent over his guard, the off tackle slides inside and protects that area.

Slamming the first defender inside first, the off end releases and heads upfield inside the wide deep defender. He may use a running shoulder block or cross-body block to hinder that opponent.

The quarterback reverses out, goes straight back, and slips the ball into the pocket formed by the halfback. He then rolls, drops, or chases.

The fullback drives hard into the 3-hole area. He fakes taking the ball by clamping his pocket and running all out—exactly as though the ball were in his possession. As soon as he crosses the line of scrimmage, he quickly turns inside to block the pursuit by the backer away from our slot side.

The halfback comes straight across, receives the ball from the quarterback, and continues toward the sideline. As soon as he gets to the play target area, he cuts squarely up into the line of scrimmage, picks up his lead blocker, and heads upfield.

Coaching Points

While the slot back is jab-stepping to allow his end to cross, he must stay low and as much out of sight as possible. He must also watch the actions of the defensive tackle. These actions will govern his play as he advances in knowledge and technique to combat various defensive moves to be seen later. Because he runs the ball in the quick counter or scissors play, and on the long reverse, the more out of sight he can be the better the chances for a successful run.

The fullback must fake realistically. The more convincing he is the more slowly the defense will react to the play at the corner. Furthermore, if the defensive tackle and linebacker are convinced they are looking at an inside buck by the fullback, our blockers will open the off-tackle area more easily.

The halfback, too, must enter into this deception. As soon as he gets the ball, he must clamp it with both hands and arms and dip his inside shoulder. This dip will hide the ball from the backer and the concerned defensive linemen and, also, for a time at least, from the corner defender. When the defense cannot find the ball, their reactions are slowed and the play has a greater chance for success.

RED 40–DIP

When the defense becomes committed to stopping 41-Square, and is bringing its defensive in hard and tight to help close off the off-tackle hole, the offense is ready to counter this move by going outside that crashing end with Red 40-Dip (Figures 3-12, 3-13, 3-14, 3-15).

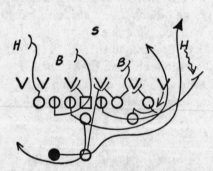

Figure 3-12
Red 40-Dip Versus 6-2 Defense

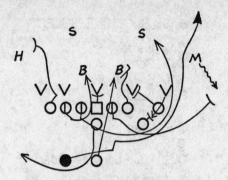

Figure 3-13
Red 40-Dip Versus 5-2 Defense

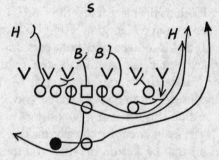

Figure 3-14
Red 40-Dip Versus 4-4 or Split-6 Defense

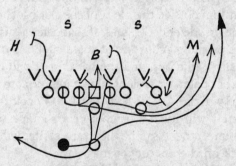

Figure 3-15
Red 40-Dip Versus 4-3 or 6-1 Defense

BASE BLOCKING RULES

S.E. Inside
S.B. Corner
S.T. Backer
S.G. Lead
  C. On; away
O.G. Lead
O.T. Fill
O.E. Wide deep defender

Position Play

Exactly as in 41-Square, in 40-Dip the slot end blocks the first inside defender. He aims his head across the crotch of that defender and, above all, denies him penetration. After his initial hit, he may use a reverse crab block to keep him from pursuit.

The slot back, after taking his jab step (which allows just enough time for the defensive crashing end to get in tight), now turns outside and uses a cross-body block to knock that defender down. He hits up from his original low position.

"Backer" is the assignment for the slot tackle. He quickly gets outside position on that backer on his side, and uses a shoulder or cross-body block to keep him from attacking the ball carrier.

The slot guard is a lead blocker. He pulls on an arc deep enough to get him outside the block of the slot back, turns upfield, and blocks the first defender he sees. If that defender is coming wide to protect the crashing end, the slot guard applies a running shoulder block to drive him out, and the ball carrier will cut up inside. However, if that defender is slow in arriving, or coming up inside, the slot guard will use a cross-body block to knock him down.

The center will use a near foot-near shoulder block on any defender on him. If there is none there, the center will use a reverse shoulder block on the first opponent away.

The off guard is another lead blocker. He, too, pulls a deep arc to get around the corner, and then immediately looks and turns up inside to cut off the first defender he sees.

"Fill" is the job of the off tackle. He must pull and protect the area left by the pulling guard. If there is an opponent over his guard, the tackle will fill the hole left by the away blocking center. If there is no opponent on his guard, the tackle will glide inside and prevent any penetration.

As usual, the off end slams the first man inside, releases and turns upfield to block the wide deep defender.

In this play, the fullback must fill the area vacated by the pulling of the slot guard. If a defender is covering that guard, the fullback will block that man. If no defender is in that spot, the fullback will go through the vacated area, turn inside, and look to block the off-side backer coming across.

The quarterback reverses out, comes straight back, slips the ball to the running back, and assumes one of his postures.

The halfback comes straight across and takes the ball. Now, however, as soon as he secures the ball, he slants inside toward the line of scrimmage as though running a slant play. As he makes this dip he picks up his lead blockers, swings back and wide, and begins his sweep around the end.

Coaching Points

As he takes his jab step, the slot back, as always, must keep low. In this case it keeps him in good blocking position from which to attack the incoming defensive end. If the slot back can hit his man from down to up, it will almost certainly knock the defender off his feet and the way will be cleared for turning the corner.

Both lead blockers are aiming at turning the corner at the block of the slot back. However, the off guard must turn upfield at the first opportunity he sees in order to quickly cut off the secondary pursuit. The slot guard must be ready to block out on the defender as he is coming in straight or gliding outside.

In addition, the halfback must run his course into the line of scrimmage exactly as though running a slant play. This will help bring in the end to the block by the slot back.

RED 26–SCISSORS

Up to this point we have been hitting the slot side-inside, outside; inside, outside. When the defenders begin to react to this concentration to the strength of the formation, it is time to switch the attack elsewhere. The first of these counter plays is Red 26-Scissors. This is an extremely fast inside reverse which, at its inception, looks exactly like the strong-side attack (Figures 3-16, 3-17, 3-18, 3-19).

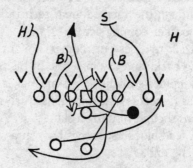

Figure 3-16
Red 26-Scissors Versus 6-2 Defense

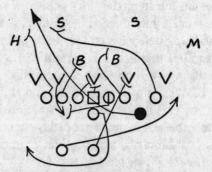

Figure 3-17
Red 26-Scissors Versus 5-2 Defense

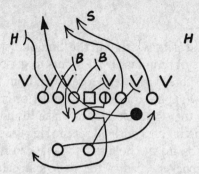

Figure 3-18
Red 26-Scissors Versus 4-4 or Split-6 Defense

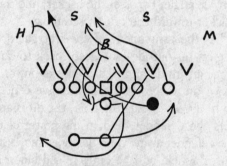

Figure 3-19
Red 26-Scissors Versus 4-3 or 6-1 Defense

BASE BLOCKING RULES

S.E. Inside deep defender
S.T. Backer
S.G. Trapper
  C. On; away
O.G. Inside
O.T. Backer
O.E. Side deep defender

Position Play

The slot end gets swiftly off the line and sprints a parallel course to the line of scrimmage. He wants to get outside the deep inside defender before that defender recovers from the initial flow. The slot end now applies a running shoulder or cross-body block.

In this play the slot back does not take his usual jab step. He wants to get to the hit area with all speed. He pushes off his outside foot and sprints toward the hole as fast as he can run. En route he forms the usual pocket, clamps the ball, and cuts up inside the block of the slot guard. Then he picks up his downfield blockers and sprints for the goal.

The slot tackle must block the linebacker on his side. He sprints for an inside angle, bypasses the backer, and then turns back to drive the backer toward the line of scrimmage.

"Trapper" is the assignment of the slot guard. He pivots a 45-degree angle on his outside foot, steps back toward the line of scrimmage to get an inside angle, and blocks out on the first defender who shows on, or beyond, the offensive center. If that defender drops to his knees to plug the hole, the off guard drops to his knees, smothers the defender, and, using powerful thrusts of his thighs, rolls the defender away. If no defender shows, the slot guard immediately turns upfield and becomes a lead blocker.

If covered, the center posts the player over him, and together with the off guard, drives that defender laterally toward the slot side. If no player is across from him, the center blocks the first opponent to the slot side. In this he uses his outside shoulder, and gets his head across that defender's crotch. The center must prevent penetration.

The off guard's rule is "inside." He blocks the first defender inside him toward the slot side. He, too, must prevent penetration.

The backer is the assignment of the off tackle. If that backer is moving in the direction of the original flow, the off tackle keeps him going in that direction. If the defender is not in movement, the off tackle, using his inside shoulder, drives the defender back to create running room for the ball carrier.

The off end slams the first man inside, sets a course inside the side deep defender, and uses a running shoulder block, or cross-body block, to keep the defender from the ball carrier.

The quarterback very quickly reverses in a 315-degree turn and hands the ball up to the slot back, who is coming full tilt. He then continues to sprint wide to the slot side.

The fullback must fill the area vacated by the slot tackle. Accordingly, he heads full speed to block the first defender on, or beyond, that area.

The halfback sprints a course parallel to the line of scrimmage. He continues on wide and keeps pace with his quarterback. He would be in position for a lateral if the quarterback had kept the ball!

Coaching Points

This scissors play must be run with all speed. The quarter-back's pivot must be extremely fast because he will be handing up to the slot back almost before he is through pivoting!

Furthermore, the fullback, who is filling the area vacated by the slot tackle, must do so in a hurry. He must beat both the quarterback and the slot back as they approach at high speed. In some cases it has been necessary to "cheat" the fullback a little closer to the line.

The scissors action in this play hides the slot back from the defense and, as he pops from behind the fullback, he very often gets through the line of scrimmage unseen. Therein lies the secret of the play. As far as the defense is concerned, almost from nowhere, a ball carrier is loose in their secondary!

RED 29-REVERSE

The next play aimed at the off side is Red 29-Reverse. This does not hit as quickly as does the previous scissors play, but it is very effective when the defense against the off side has become careless and the secondary pursuit very quick (Figures 3-20, 3-21, 3-22, 3-23).

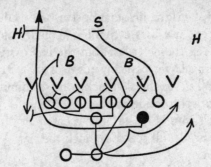

Figure 3-20
Red 29-Reverse Versus 6-2 Defense

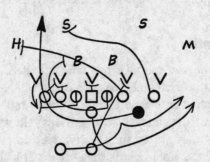

Figure 3-21
Red 29-Reverse Versus 5-2 Defense

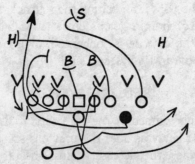

Figure 3-22
Red 29-Reverse Versus 4-4 or Split-6 Defense

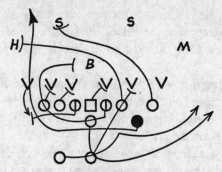

Figure 3-23
Red 29-Reverse Versus 4-3 or 6-1 Defense

BASE BLOCKING RULES

S.E. Inside deep defender
S.T. Off side deep wide
S.G. Off backer
C. On; away
O.G. Corner
O.T. On; inside
O.E. Inside

Position Play

The slot end, who is responsible for the inside deep defender, sprints a flat course parallel to the line of scrimmage to get outside position. He then applies a running shoulder block or cross-body block to keep that player from the ball carrier.

The slot tackle sprints across the field heading for the wide deep defender on the off side. Since he already has good inside position, the slot tackle uses a running shoulder block to drive that defender toward the sidelines.

Using a reverse pivot, the slot guard pulls to the off side, turns up inside the block of the off guard, looks inside and blocks the off backer. He may use a shoulder or cross-body block.

If a defender is covering the center, the center uses his slot-side shoulder to drive him down the line of scrimmage. He must then work around him to prevent recovery and pursuit. If the center is uncovered, he blocks the first defender to the slot side. He must prevent penetration as he drives his head beyond the opponent's crotch and his away shoulder to drive. He must prevent penetration.

Also using a reverse pivot, the off guard, keeping close to the line of scrimmage, blocks out on the first defender to show on, or beyond, the off end. He will hit with his closest shoulder and drive the opponent toward the sidelines.

The off tackle, if covered, post blocks the defender on him. Together with the off end, he is using a post-and-drive block. In this combination block, the tackle must prevent penetration and the end will furnish the drive. If uncovered, the tackle blocks the first man inside by driving his head beyond that player's crotch, hitting with his outside shoulder, and driving the defender down the line. He must not let that defender penetrate across the line of scrimmage.

The off end, who has been preparing for this play by slamming the first defender inside on every play, is now prepared to "two-hit" that opponent. He first steps inside with his close foot and delivers a quick "hit" with the corresponding forearm. Now, he quickly brings back his inside foot, drives from his outside foot, and thrusts his head and shoulders across the defender's middle. He is now in what amounts to a reverse cross-body block as a result of the second "hit." On all fours, he continues to drive the defender in a lateral direction while maintaining a high bridge to prevent penetration.

The quarterback reverses out, retreats, and hands the ball off to the running back, then "chases."

The instant the running back gets the ball, he secures it with both hands, and slants toward the line of scrimmage. He must get inside the slot back, who is now approaching him. He now hands the ball back to the slot back and then continues on into the line of scrimmage.

Meantime, the fullback has driven into the line of scrimmage to block the first defender or, beyond, our slot tackle.

The slot back, who is the ball carrier, drop steps with his outside foot and simultaneously executes a head-and-shoulder fake to the outside. Then he pivots on his outside foot, reverses his direction, and takes the hand up from the halfback. Now, he cuts up inside the block at the corner, picks up his downfield blockers, and heads for the goal.

Coaching Points

The timing and coordination in this play are most important. The movements of the guards and slot back, in addition to feinting a slot-side play, also work out the timing so that these blockers, and the ball carrier, do not get to the point of attack too soon.

Both guards first pivot on the foot away from the slot side and step out with the closest foot as though pulling for a run to the slot side. They must keep their weight in balance and their bodies low, and they must be facing the sideline. Now, they pivot on the advance foot, and turn back inside 180 degrees so that they are now facing the off sideline. They are now ready to run their assignments. This reverse pivot must be fluid, and, above all, the guards must stay low.

The slot back drops his outside foot, keeps low, and turns his trunk to face the sidelines. He is doing exactly what the guards are doing and in the same rhythm. Now, he, too, makes a 180-degree turn, takes the hand back from the halfback, and cuts up into the hole.

RED 10–KEEPER

The last play in the Red series is 10-Keeper. This is an out-side reverse with the ball being "bootlegged" by the quarterback. It is a good play to use when the off defensive end is coming in tight to chase a play to the slot side (Figures 3-24, 3-25, 3-26, 3-27).

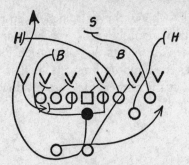

Figure 3-24
Red 10-Keeper Versus 6-2 Defense

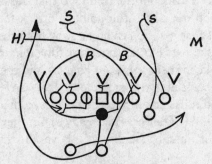

Figure 3-25
Red 10-Keeper Versus 5-2 Defense

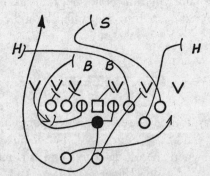

Figure 3-26
Red 10-Keeper Versus 4-4 or Split-6 Defense

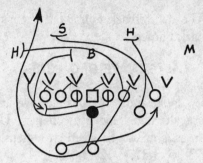

Figure 3-27
Red 10-Keeper Versus 4-3 or 6-1 Defense

BASE BLOCKING RULES

S.E. Inside deep defender
S.B. Wide deep defender
S.T. Off side deep wide
S.G. Off backer
C. On; away
O.G. Corner
O.T. On; inside
O.E. Inside

Position Play

The line play is exactly like that in 29-Reverse with the single exception of the off guard. Now, because the play is going outside against a close-playing defensive end, the off guard uses a chop block, or a cross-body block, to down that end. The slot back is blocking downfield.

Coaching Points

With the two exceptions noted, they are exactly the same as in 29-Reverse. Moreover, the quarterback must hide the ball behind his back leg as he fakes on all "roll." And, in the beginning, he must not suddenly put on a sudden burst of speed. The whole action must be the exact picture seen in any slot-side play where the roll is chosen. The quarterback must "lull them to sleep" before turning on the back burners.

ALTERNATE BLOCKING

To get a new look, and to make defensive keys a little more unreliable, we use alternate blocking schemes. Usually, this involves a switch in assignments between two offensive players (Figures 3-28, 3-29, 3-30, 3-31, 3-32, 3-33).

This, of course, is isolation blocking, and involves a very simple exchange in blocking responsibilities.

Here again a simple change in blocking assignments has given us an alternate method of attacking the defense.

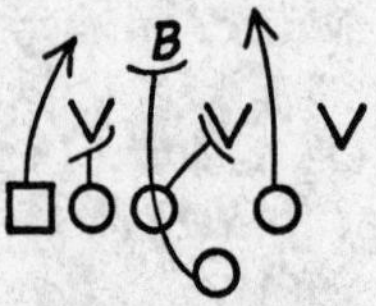

Figure 3-28
Red 33-Drive Versus Even Defense

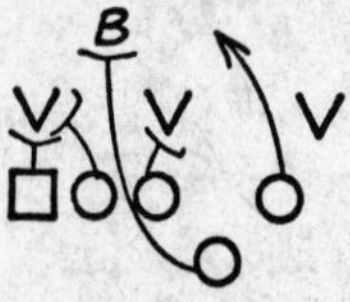

Figure 3-29
Red 33-Drive Versus Old Defense

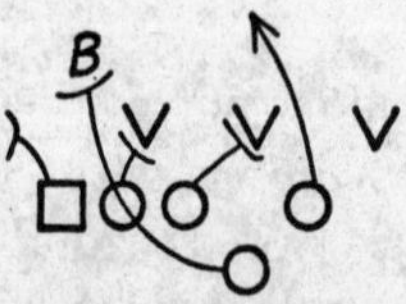

Figure 3-30
Red 33-Drive Versus Gap Defense

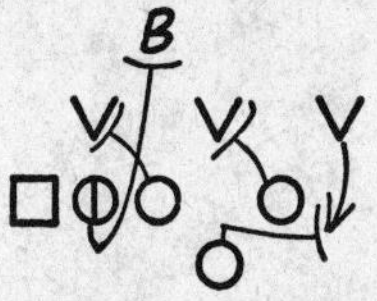

**Figure 3-31
Red 41-Square Versus Even Defense**

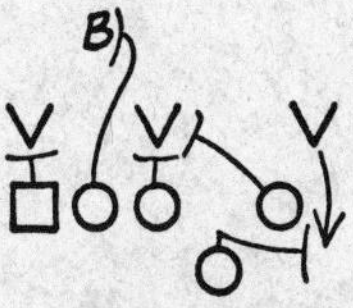

**Figure 3-32
Red 41-Square Versus Odd Defense**

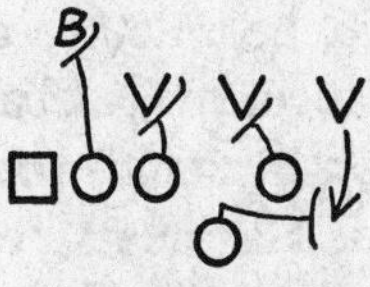

**Figure 3-33
Red 41-Square Versus Gap Defense**

AUTOMATIC BLOCKING

There are some defenses that require immediate adjustments on the line of scrimmage if the play is to be run successfully. Most common are the gap stack and tandem stacks. To meet these we make the following adjustments automatically (Figures 3-34, 3-35).

The defender in the gap is driven straight back by the slot guard and slot tackle. The center or the slot back picks off the linebacker when he comes toward one or the other.

Usually, in a stunting defense, the on lineman and backer will stunt in opposite directions. The slot guard aims at the midsection of the defender across from him, and stays with him. He must prevent penetration. The center and slot tackle drive at the closest shoulder of that same defender. Now, if that player slants to his

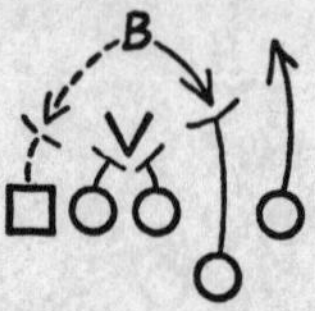

Figure 3-34
Red 33-Drive Versus Gap Stack

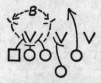

Figure 3-35
Red 33-Drive Versus Tandem Stack

outside, he is caught in a double-team block by the slot guard and slot tackle; if he slants inside, he is double-teamed by the slot guard and center. In the first instance, the linebacker is picked off by the slot tackle, and in the second instance, by the center.

Because of our slot-side alignment, we have not encountered stacks or tandems wider than our 3-hole area. However we do see slants and loops to that side.

BLOCKING SLANTS AND LOOPS

In the interest of simplicity, we consider slants and loops as identical maneuvers using slightly different techniques. As a rule, the defensive line is going one way and the backers are covering away from the charge. Consequently, we simply regard all of these movements as slants (Figures 3-36 through 3-41).

In every case the out charge by the defender in the slot-tackle area is, by going outside, an easy mark for the cross blocking guard—and the inside defender is coming into the block by the slot tackle.

Once again the slant charge is opening the hole on the inside and the slot guard, who is blocking outside, has a defender coming into his block.

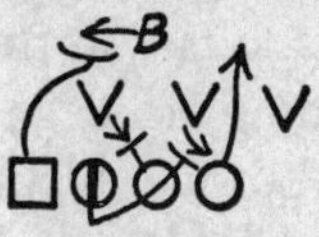

Figure 3-36
Red 33-X Versus Out Slant by 6-2 Defense

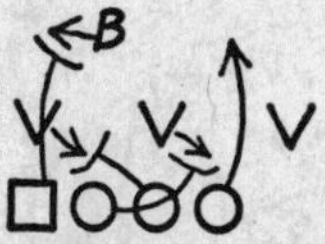

Figure 3-37
Red 33-X Versus Out Slant by 5-2 Defense

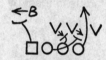

Figure 3-38
Red 33-X Versus Out Slant by Gap Defense

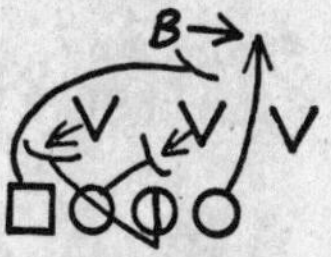

Figure 3-39
Red 33-X Versus In Charge by 6-2 Defense

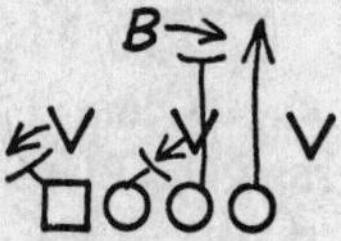

Figure 3-40
Red 33-X Versus In Charge by 5-2 Defense

Figure 3-41
Red 33-X Versus In Charge by Gap Defense

In blocking slants, in and out, at the 1 hole, the slot back has a special rule: "If the defending tackle goes inside, go with him and keep him going; if he goes outside, block the backer." As the slot back takes his usual jab step, he has the time to key the defending tackle and to adjust his block accordingly (Figures 3-42, 3-43, 3-44, 3-45).

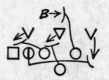

Figure 3-42
Red 41-Square Versus In Slant by 6-2 Defense

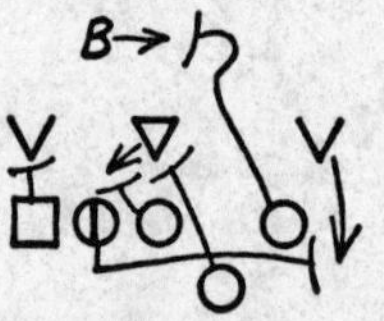

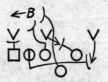

Figure 3-43
Red 41-Square Versus In Slant by 5-2 Defense

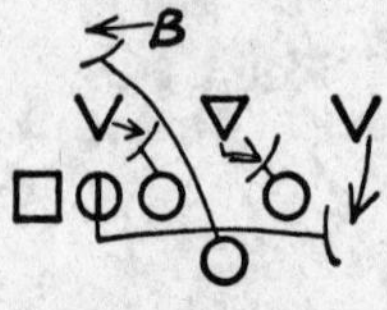

Figure 3-44
Red 41-Square Versus Out Slant by 6-2 Defense

Figure 3-45
Red 41-Square Versus Out Slant by 5-2 Defense

In both instances, the slot back has applied his rule in going with the in slant of the defending tackle. The slot end, seeing his inside target disappearing, adjusts to blocking the backer.

Now, as the slot back sees his key going outside, he immediately switches his target to the backer, who, protecting inside, is not a difficult target. Meanwhile, the slot end blocks his inside defender who, in this slant, is coming at him.

BLOCKING BLITZES

We have not been too concerned with blitzing to the slot side of our formation. If we are running 41-Square and the backer comes inside, he will be met by the fullback, and, if he is going outside, he will be blocked by the slot back. If we are running 33-X and the defense is showing a strong tendency to blitz on that side, we will switch to alternate blocking and isolate that backer to the block of our slot back.

4

The White Series in the Tight-Slot Attack

HOW TO ATTACK THE OFF SIDE

The White Series attacks the defense with speed and deception, using plays that are run away from the set of the slot back. This tends to keep the defensive team from ganging up to the side of the set. The ever-present threat of the explosive off-side capability keeps them honest.

WHITE 47–DRIVE

The base play in this series is White 47-Drive. It is the halfback quick hitter and, in addition to setting up the other plays of the series, it is very often a long gainer in its own right (Figures 4-1, 4-2, 4-3, 4-4).

BASE BLOCKING RULES

S.E. Inside deep defender
S.B. Wide deep defender

S.T. On; backer
S.G. On; backer
 C. On; backer
O.G. On; backer
O.T. On; outside
O.E. Wide deep defender

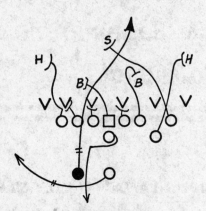

Figure 4-1
White 47-Drive Versus 6-2 Defense

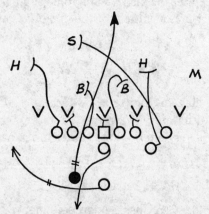

Figure 4-2
White 47-Drive Versus 5-2 Defense

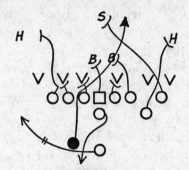

Figure 4-3
White 47-Drive Versus 4-4 or Split-6 Defense

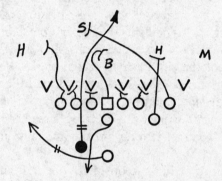

Figure 4-4
White 47-Drive Versus 4-3 or 6-1 Defense

Position Play

The slot end sprints off the line and heads for the defender in the deep inside area. He times his run and sets his course to arrive at that defender as the ball carrier makes his cut away from the flow of the play. At this point the slot end applies a running shoulder block and drives the defender away from the path of the ball carrier. In making this block, his target is the numbers on the defender's jersey. If, for any reason, he cannot apply a shoulder block, a cross-body block is used. Now the target is the opponent's midsection, and the slot back throws his closest hip there, keeping his leg on that side extended. He is building a bridge between the defender and the runner.

The slot back jab steps to allow his end to clear, and then sets a course that will bring him inside the wide deep defender. Once there, he applies a running shoulder block, and drives the defender toward the sideline. He, too, if necessary, may bridge with a cross-body block.

The slot tackle, if covered, uses his outside shoulder to drive his opponent to the outside. He continues to work around him to prevent his getting into the pursuit by rolling back into the running lane. If the slot tackle is uncovered, he releases from the line on an inside angle that will take him beyond the backer. He wants to get deeper than his opponent so that he can block him back toward the line of scrimmage. This prevents the backer from falling off into the path of the ball carrier who is cutting back to that side.

The play of the slot guard is like that of the slot tackle. If covered, he uses his outside shoulder to drive his opponent away from the running lane, and works around him to cut off his pursuit. When the slot guard is uncovered, he bypasses his opponent, and then turns back to drive him toward the line of scrimmage for the same reason.

The center, if he finds an opponent over him, uses the shoulder that is away from the hole to drive his opponent in a lateral direction. In so doing he creates a larger area in which the ball carrier can make his cut away from the flow. If no one is playing on him, the center blocks the play-side linebacker. He gets off the line quickly, and uses a running shoulder block to drive the defender toward the sideline.

The off guard, when playing a defender across from him, uses his inside shoulder to drive his opponent in a lateral direction. He continues to work around him to keep him from getting a pursuit angle. When no defender is over the guard, he takes an inside route to get into position to drive the backer away toward the sideline.

The off tackle, if covered, uses his outside shoulder to drive his opponent in a lateral direction. With no defender over him, the off tackle blocks the first player to his outside. He takes a short, lateral outside step and watches the play of the defender. If that player is coming down the line of scrimmage at him, the off tackle uses his outside shoulder to drive the defender out. If the defender is crossing deep, the offensive tackle moves laterally, and now uses his inside shoulder to block. In this reverse shoulder block the off tackle must aim at the defender's crotch to make certain that he gets his head by the defender.

The off end, before making his approach to the deep outside defender, must "influence block" the first defender to his inside on the line of scrimmage. To do this, he steps toward that man with his inside foot, and delivers a slam with the forearm on the same side. The off end must always make that defender aware of outside pressure. Then the off end releases and runs a course inside the deep defender. He applies a running shoulder block, or a cross-body block, to remove that opponent.

The quarterback reverse pivots to the off side. He holds the ball close to his abdomen with both hands. He slips the ball into the pocket formed by the running back with the hand that is closer to the line of scrimmage, fakes a pitch to the flaring fullback, and then retreats to an area about 7 yards behind the position of the off tackle. He then sets up as though preparing to throw.

The halfback, eyes on the hitting area, forms a pocket for the ball by placing his outside arm and hand—palm up—across his midsection at belt level. His inside arm—with hand palm down—is held across his chest and parallel to the ground. As soon as the halfback feels the ball, he clamps it with his hand and forearms and drives into the hole. He does not look at the quarterback, but concentrates on the in-line blocking and the blocks on the backers. He is always aware that he wants to cut back toward the slot side to pick up the deep downfield blockers.

As the ball is snapped, the fullback, using a cross-over step, opens away from the line of scrimmage, gains depth, and continues to swing wide. He is looking at the quarterback, and as the quarterback begins his pitch motions, the fullback extends his arms and hands exactly as though he were going to catch the ball. He keeps swinging wide.

It is the slot back's job to keep any defender from crashing to his inside. He steps laterally with his inside foot and is ready to block any opponent trying to cross in front of him.

Coaching Points

The quarterback, in reversing out, first takes a short step back with his outside foot, pivots on the ball of that foot, and spins a 135-degree arc. His turn stops as his opposite foot is planted at a 45-degree angle to the line of scrimmage. He must keep his torso erect and head back to avoid a collision with the diving halfback, and to allow that back to run a straight course into the hitting area. It is the sole responsibility of the quarterback to place the ball correctly at belt level into the pocket formed by the runner.

The halfback must never look for the ball. He must fix his eyes on the hole area and the action taking place there so that he can quickly adjust to what he sees.

The fullback must be sure to use a cross-over start as he begins his swing because that is the identical movement he will make in running 38-X and 39-Pitch.

WHITE 38–X

The next play in our White Series is 38-X. It starts exactly like 47-Drive, and is used when the defensive tackle starts to charge hard to his inside to stop that play (Figures 4-5, 4-6, 4-7, 4-8).

BASE BLOCKING RULES

S.E. Inside deep defender
S.B. Area
S.T. On; backer
S.G. On; backer
 C. On; side deep defender
O.G. On; side deep defender
O.T. Corner
O.E. Inside

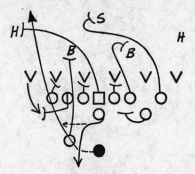

Figure 4-5
White 38-X Versus 6-2 Defense

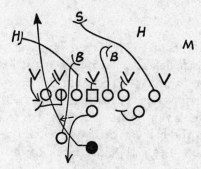

Figure 4-6
White 38-X Versus 5-2 Defense

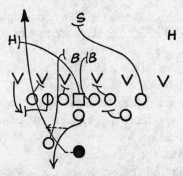

Figure 4-7
White 38-X Versus 4-4 or Split-6 Defense

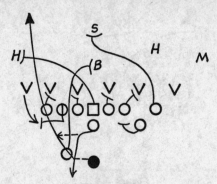

Figure 4-8
White 38-X Versus 4-3 or 6-1 Defense

Position Play

The slot end flies off the line on a flat angle that will get him inside the deep inside defender. He must run fast and parallel to the line of scrimmage in order to beat that defender to the running lane. If that player has not yet reached the lane, the slot end will turn upfield and use a running shoulder block or a cross-body block to keep him from the ball carrier. However, if the defender beats him there, he now uses a shoulder block to drive the defender toward the sideline.

The slot back blocks area. He must see that no defender crashes to his inside.

The slot tackle, if covered, uses his outside shoulder to block the defender out, and continues to work around him to deny pursuit. If uncovered, the slot tackle takes an inside course to get inside the backer and applies either a shoulder or cross-body block.

The guard on the slot side, finding an opponent over him, uses an inside-out block with his outside shoulder and continues to work around that opponent to keep him out of the pursuit. If he finds no defender on him, he releases to get inside the backer and blocks him away from the play area.

If an opponent is aligned over the center, the center will use his shoulder away from the hole to drive that defender away from the path of the ball. The center will work around him to keep him from getting into the pursuit. If no player is lined up over the center, he will quickly release through the line of scrimmage, set a course inside the play-side deep defender, and use a shoulder block or cross-body block to drive the defender away from the running lane.

The off guard, with a player over him, uses his inside shoulder to drive the defender laterally, and then works around him to keep him from chasing the play. If no defender is over the off guard, he will release through the line of scrimmage, "influence" the backer, and set a course inside the deep-side defender. He then applies a running shoulder or cross-body block.

The responsibility of the off tackle is "corner." He blocks out on the first defender showing outside his own off end. He pulls tight to the line of scrimmage to get an inside-out approach angle on that defender. If the defender is coming hard, the off tackle will use his outside shoulder to drive the defender to the outside. However, if that player is crossing deep, the off tackle uses his inside shoulder to execute a reverse shoulder block. In both cases, the target for the off tackle is the numbers on the opponent's jersey. As soon as contact is made, the off tackle quickly slides his block up so that he screens the defender's vision.

The off end must block the first player inside. He drives off his outside foot, gets his head across the defender, and uses his outside shoulder to drive that defender down the line of scrimmage. He cannot allow that defender to penetrate.

The quarterback executes the same reverse pivot as in 47-Drive. As the halfback drives by, the quarterback, keeping both hands on the ball—and not extending it—fakes the handoff by a slight dip with his inside shoulder. As soon as the halfback clears, the quarterback locates the fullback—who is now heading into the line of scrimmage—and softly tosses the ball to him. He then retreats as though to pass.

The halfback drives into the line of scrimmage as fast as he can sprint. He watches the backer on that side and must keep him from the running lane. As he passes the quarterback, his arms and hands forming the usual pocket, he drops his upper arm exactly as though taking the ball.

The fullback uses a cross-over step to get under way. Then as soon as his outside foot touches the ground, he turns upfield at 45 degrees, and is ready to catch the toss from the quarterback. As soon as he has secured the ball, he shoots into the hole, locates his downfield blockers, and heads for the goal.

Coaching Points

In running 38-X, it is important that it look exactly like 47-Drive. The play-side backer must be convinced that that is what he is seeing. Accordingly, the shoulder fake by the quarterback and the take fake by the halfback must be convincing. This allows the halfback to get good position for his block. When the play is well executed, the backer often tackles the halfback, and this removes him as a threat to the runner.

The fullback, as he takes his cross-over step, must keep low and actually face the sideline. He must not look for the ball until he makes his cut to the hole. His movements must be fluid; he must look as though he is making a wide swing.

The off tackle, who is blocking inside-out on the end man must hit and raise as he drives. He must screen that defender's vision.

WHITE 39–PITCH

When 38-X has been established, and the end defender starts to fight hard inside to stop it, the stage is set for 39-Pitch. This play is designed to get outside the perimeter without actually blocking the end man. The ball is pitched wide and run around him while he is being "entertained" by the actions of the off tackle who is simulating 38-X (Figures 4-9, 4-10, 4-11, 4-12).

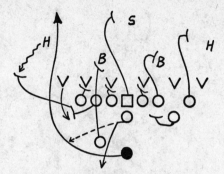

Figure 4-9
White 39-Pitch Versus 6-2 Defense

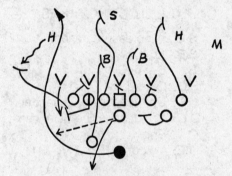

Figure 4-10
White 39-Pitch Versus 5-2 Defense

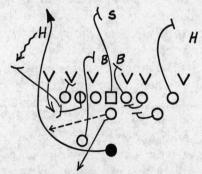

Figure 4-11
White 39-Pitch Versus 4-4 or Split-6 Defense

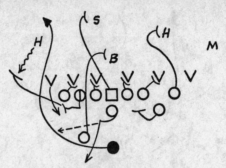

Figure 4-12
White 39-Pitch Versus 4-3 or 6-1 Defense

BASE BLOCKING RULES

S.E.	Wide deep defender
S.B.	Area
S.T.	On; backer
S.G.	On; backer
C.	On; deep inside defender
O.G.	On; deep inside defender
O.T.	Entertain
O.E.	Inside

Position Play

The slot end flies off the line on an angle that gets him well inside the deep-side defender. He then sets so that defender—to attack the ball carrier—must run through his position. He then applies a shoulder or cross-body block.

The slot back blocks the area and prevents any defender from crashing inside his position and getting to the quarterback.

The slot tackle, if covered, attacks that defender with his outside shoulder, and works around him to keep him out of the pursuit. If there is no player on him, the slot tackle takes a course through the line of scrimmage that will place him between the backer and the path of the ball carrier. He uses a shoulder or cross-body block to keep the backer out of the run area.

The slot guard has the same responsibilities as the slot tackle.

If the guard is opposed by an opponent on the line of scrimmage, he attacks him with his outside shoulder, works around him, and keeps him from the pursuit. If there is no defender on him, he takes an inside approach to the backer, and applies a shoulder or cross-body block.

The center is responsible for any player over him on the line of scrimmage. If there is a defender in that area, the center blocks with his shoulder away from the hole, and works around him to keep him from falling off into the pursuit. If no defender is covering him on the line of scrimmage, the center sprints to the play-side deep-inside defender, and takes a position that will force that defender to run through him to get to the ball carrier. He uses a shoulder or cross-body block.

The responsibility of the off guard is exactly that of the center. When he is opposed on the line of scrimmage, he uses his inside shoulder to force the defender away from the hole and then works around him to keep him out of the pursuit. When the off guard is uncovered, he blocks the defender in the deep middle area.

"Entertain" is the base blocking rule for the off tackle. His objective is to get the attention of the defensive end man long enough so that the ball can be pitched by him while he is still concerned with the apparent inside-out block off the off tackle. Accordingly, the off tackle pulls close to the line of scrimmage so that he can get an inside position on the defending end man. He aims for the numbers on that opponent's jersey and places a high shoulder block on those numbers just as though he were blocking 38-X. He is convincing the end defender that the play is being run inside. It is at this point—as the defender is fighting back to protect the inside—that the ball is pitched wide outside. Moreover, the high block at the numbers has obstructed the view of the defender. Quickly, now, the off tackle releases inside, takes a flat course outside, and prepares to attack the approaching deep-side defender.

The off end blocks the first defender inside. He must prevent penetration so he aims his head across the crotch of the defender and drives him with his outside shoulder.

The quarterback reverses out and makes a quick, underhand

pitch to his fullback. He does not fake to the diving halfback because he is getting the ball out to the fullback as quickly as possible.

The halfback drives into the line of scrimmage as though running 47-Drive. He stays low, fakes taking the ball by clamping his arms together, and proceeds through the line to block the linebacker.

Crossing over at top speed, the fullback looks immediately for the ball, which will arrive with some zip on it. He expects the ball at the precise instant that he is in a position in back of—but in line with—the position of the end defender while that defender is being entertained by the off tackle. The fullback catches the ball, heads upfield at full speed, and looks for the block on the deep-side defender.

Coaching Points

It is vital to train the quarterback in the correct footwork. Pitching, when reversing left, requires a special technique. After completing his 135-degree turn and stopping with his right foot at a 45-degree angle to the line of scrimmage, the quarterback now steps out on the same angle with his left foot, brings the toe of his right foot to the heel of his left, steps out again with his left foot and releases the ball with an underhand pitch. The "stutter step" synchronizes his foot and arm movements so that he can smoothly deliver the ball.

Pitching after reversing right is a simpler movement. After completing his spin, the quarterback glides his right toe to the heel of his left foot, steps out again with his left foot, and pitches the ball.

In both cases, it is important that the quarterback keep his knee close to the ground as he delivers the ball. This helps put the ball on a rising plane and makes it easier to catch.

The off tackle, if the end defender is crashing hard and tight, may take him down with a chop block. If that defender is shuffling to the outside, the off tackle may keep him going and the ball carrier will cut up inside.

WHITE 44–TRAP

The final play in the White Series is 44-Trap. It is a quick counter play, and is called when the defensive team is overcommitting to the flow of the earlier plays. It is very often an extremely long gainer (Figures 4-13, 4-14, 4-15, 4-16).

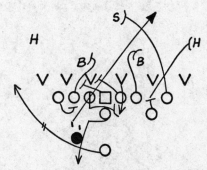

Figure 4-13
White 44-Trap Versus 6-2 Defense

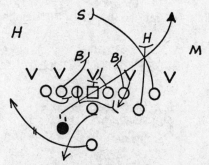

Figure 4-14
White 44-Trap Versus 5-2 Defense

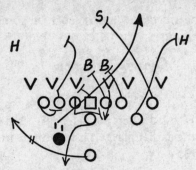

Figure 4-15
White 44-Trap Versus 4-4 or Split-6 Defense

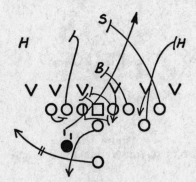

Figure 4-16
White 44-Trap Versus 4-3 or 6-1 Defense

BASE BLOCKING RULES

S.E. Inside deep defender
S.B. Side deep defender
S.T. Backer
S.G. Inside
   C. On; away
O.G. Trapper
O.T. Backer
O.E. Inside cut off

Position Play

The slot end releases on a course to close off the middle of the deep defense from the path of the ball carrier. He uses a running shoulder block or cross-body block to eliminate that defender.

Jab-stepping, to allow the slot end to clear, the slot back takes an inside route to the side of the wide deep defender in order to keep him from the ball carrier. He takes a position that will make the deep-side defender run through him to get at the runner. He uses a shoulder block or cross-body block to keep the running lane clear.

The slot tackle, covered or uncovered, blocks the backer on his side. When possible he takes an inside course to cut off the defender. However, if that defender is on the move toward the flow, the slot tackle drives him from behind across the hole area. This is perfectly legal and in accord with the rules governing close-line play.

The slot guard blocks the first man inside. Against an even defense, he is the power blocker in a power-chute combination. If the defense is set with a player over the center, the slot guard is the drive blocker in a power-post combination. And, in some cases, his target is the opposite backer.

The center posts any player on the line of scrimmage in front of him by driving into his midsection and preventing him from penetrating. At the same time, the slot guard will be driving on the same defender, and, together, they drive the defender laterally to create a running lane. If there is no player in front of him, the center drives away on the first defender away from the slot side.

The off guard is the trapper. He drop steps at 45-degrees with his inside foot, and looks for the first defender showing beyond his center. He proceeds to block that defender with his inside shoulder. In his approach, the off guard must take an inside-out course close to the line of scrimmage so that he will have a good blocking angle. He is not looking for a specific opponent—simply the first defender who penetrates. If none does penetrate, the off guard heads up into the running lane, and then blocks the first defender he sees.

Covered or uncovered, the off tackle blocks the closest linebacker. If possible, he gets inside a wide backer and drives him outside. If the backer is going the other way, the off tackle drives him across the hole.

In 44-Trap, the off end has a new assignment. He must cut off the first defender to his inside and prevent him from getting into the backfield. To do this, the off end must pull laterally inside with depth. He applies a high cross-body block, maintains a high bridge and prevents the defender from penetrating.

Reversing away from the slot side, the quarterback makes a quick toss fake to the flaring fullback, and then hands the ball off to the halfback.

The fullback, keeping his eyes on the quarterback, flares to the outside. As the quarterback makes his toss fake, the fullback extends his arms and hands as though to catch the ball. He continues to sprint wide.

To get under way, the halfback uses special footwork. He first takes a short jab step forward with his inside foot, and then another with his outside foot. As soon as that foot strikes the ground, he turns on it, forms the pocket, and drives into the line of scrimmage over the area of the slot guard. He cuts inside the block by his trapper, and heads upfield to pick up the blocking there.

Coaching Points

The off guard, who is trapping the first defender showing beyond his center, must take an exact 45-degree angle as he starts his pull. That places him in a position from which he can at once see any penetrating defender, and enables him to adjust his angle of approach to the defender's course. The trapper must keep low and in good balance as he drives the defender out. If that defender drops to his knees to plug the hole area, the off guard drops to his own knees and smothers the defender by throwing his body over and across him. At the same time, the trapper rolls the defender aside by vigorous thrusts of his legs and thighs.

The quarterback makes his usual reverse out. Here, however,

as he stops his turn, he draws his front foot alongside his back foot. This action allows the halfback to enter the running area without danger of tripping over the quarterback's feet.

ALTERNATE BLOCKING

The Tight-Slot attack uses alternate blocking for several reasons. First, alternate blocking schemes sometimes give better blocking results against slants and loops. Second, they give us a "new look." Defenders, especially linebackers, very often key the blocking patterns to locate the area of attack. This gives them something additional to think about.

Alternate blocking usually involves the switching of assignments by only two players on the play side. All the remaining players continue to apply base blocking rules. Illustrated below are examples of alternate blocking against an even, odd, and gap defense (Figures 4-17 through 4-25).

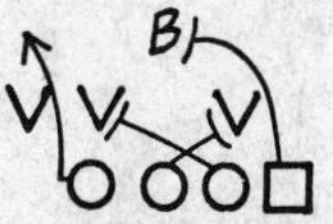

Figure 4-17
White 47-Drive Versus Even Defense

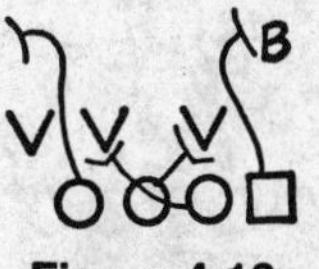

Figure 4-18
White 47-Drive Versus Odd Defense

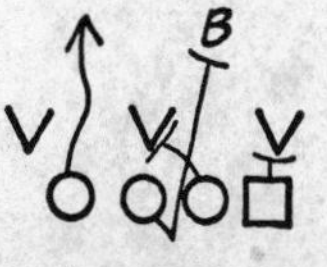

Figure 4-19
White 47-Drive Versus Gap Defense

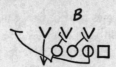

Figure 4-20
White 39-Pitch Versus Even Defense

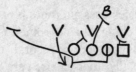

Figure 4-21
White 39-Pitch Versus Odd Defense

Figure 4-22
White 39-Pitch Versus Gap Defense

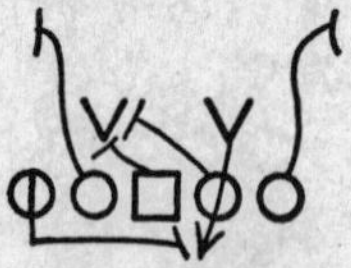

Figure 4-23
White 44-Trap Versus Even Defense

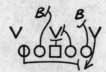

Figure 4-24
White 44-Trap Versus Odd Defense

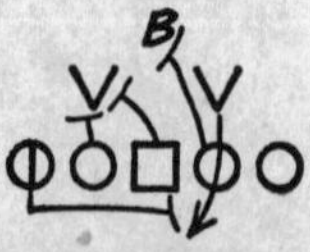

Figure 4-25
White 44-Trap Versus Gap Defense

In White 47-Drive, the base blocking of the off guard is on; backer. In alternate blocking it becomes outside. Similarly, the base blocking for the off tackle is on; outside: in alternate blocking inside; backer.

As in the previous example, alternate blocking has been accomplished merely by switching the base blocking rules for the off guard and off tackle.

Here, once more, a new blocking arrangement has been arrived at by switching the base assignments of the off guard and off tackle.

AUTOMATIC BLOCKING

The Tight-Slot attack uses automatic blocking schemes at the point of attack to counter some unusual defensive alignments. The most frequently seen are the gap stack and the tandem stack. The offense must be prepared to handle them (Figures 4-26 through 4-32).

Figure 4-26
White 47-Drive Versus Gap Stack

Figure 4-27
White 47-Drive Versus Tandem Stack

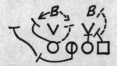

Figure 4-28
White 39-Pitch Versus Tandem Stack

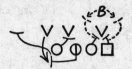

Figure 4-29
White 38-X Versus Gap Stack

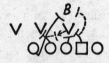

Figure 4-30
White 38-X Versus Tandem Stack

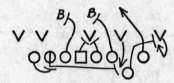

Figure 4-31
White 44-Trap Versus Gap Stack

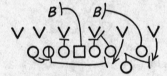

Figure 4-32
White 44-Trap Versus Tandem Stack

The defender in the gap is occupying the offensive center and the off guard, and so hopes to free the linebacker. The center and the off guard drive the gap defender straight back, and the off end folds behind his tackle to pick off the linebacker.

The tandem stack usually means a stunting game by the defender on the line and the backer behind him. Accordingly, we must be prepared to block these games. The off guard will aim at the middle of the defender aligned on him, and stay with him no matter where he goes. It is the job of the off guard to prevent that defender from penetrating the line of scrimmage. The center and the off tackle drive at the shoulder of that defender. If that man slants to his own right, he will be caught in a double-team block by the off guard and off tackle. The center, seeing the defender slant away, will go on by him and pick the backer who is coming his way. Conversely, if the defender is slanting to his own left, he will be double-teamed by the center and off guard. The off tackle will pick up the linebacker, who will be coming in his direction.

The off end steps quickly inside to pick off the player in the stack opposite him who is coming inside. Obviously, he must be alert and ready for the defender closest to him, and be prepared to play him at once. However, when that defender goes outside, the off end quickly adjusts to pick the backer who will be coming in his direction.

The off end is primarily concerned with the backer. The end steps at the defender opposite him, but makes no attempt to block. He is watching the backer. If the on-line defender comes inside, the off end will quickly widen outside to get blocking position on the backer, who will be coming in that direction. If the opponent on the line of scrimmage goes outside, the off end lets him go, and prepares to block the backer as he makes his inside move.

This set presents no problem. The off end and the off tackle execute a normal cross blocking technique, and the driving halfback picks up the backer if he is coming that way. The off guard and center double-team the gap defender, and then the center seals his side.

The tandem stack requires an adjustment. In place of the regular cross blocking movement, the off end uses a fold technique. The off tackle crosses first, and blocks the first defender showing outside. That will be the backer or the defender on the line of scrimmage opposite the off end. The off end steps behind his tackle, and moves inside to cut off the first defender he sees; either the backer or the defender playing opposite the off guard. The off guard stays with the opponent opposite him. If that defender goes inside, he goes with him and helps him along. If the defender goes outside, he goes with him and combines with his off end in a double-team block. The center blocks area.

When faced with a gap set in the hole area, we move the hole one space out and execute the long trap. This is automatic and the team is alerted by a "long" call. Now the off tackle becomes the trapper, and blocks out on the first man showing beyond the slot tackle. The center and the slot guard drive the gap defender straight back, and the slot tackle seals off the backer. The slot back influences the closest inside defender, and then turns out on the defensive end man to keep him from rolling back into the running lane. The off guard blocks the backer on his side.

Here we also have a long trap situation. We must handle the tandem stack in the hit area. We anticipate a stunt between the stacked defenders—one inside, one outside. In this tandem situation we use a "do-dad" technique; the slot guard aims at the inside hip of the defender across from him. If that defender goes inside, the guard stays with him and keeps him going. The slot tackle, who is aiming at the outside shoulder of the player over the slot guard, sees him disappear inside, and quickly adjusts to pick up the backer coming his way. On the other hand, if the defender over the slot guard is going outside, the slot guard ignores him and blocks the backer coming his way. The slot tackle blocks the lineman coming at him.

BLOCKING SLANTS AND LOOPS

To keep things simple, we regard slants and loops as the same thing. Both move linemen in one direction with backers compensating in the other. The difference, then, is one of technique. Accordingly, we always refer to these movements as slants (Figures 4-33, 4-34, 4-35).

In all instances, the defender outside the off tackle is slanting himself out of the play, and is an easy mark for the cross blocking guard. The next defender inside is coming to the off tackle, who, of course, has a fine blocking angle. The backer, in compensating for

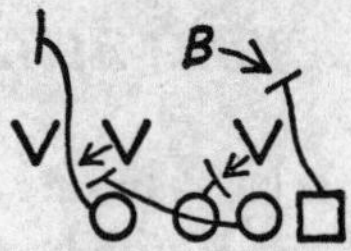

Figure 4-33
White 47-Drive Versus Out Slant by 6-2 Defense

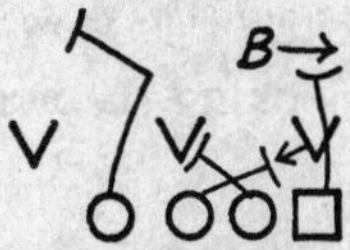

Figure 4-34
White 47-Drive Versus Out Slant by 5-2 Defense

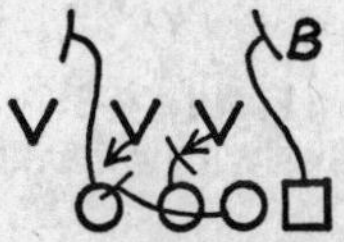

Figure 4-35
White 47-Drive Versus Out Slant by Gap Defense

the line slant, becomes an easy target for our center. This is alternate blocking, and is very effective against slants.

THE WEDGE

If, for any reason, we are having difficulty in blocking the 7-hole area against stunts, we run the play behind wedge blocking (Figure 4-36).

Defenses that are looping and slanting are susceptible to wedge blocking for the simple reason that the defense is moving in a lateral direction, and cannot readily repel the powerful forward thrust of the forward-moving wedge.

Figure 4-36
White 47-Drive with Wedge Blocking

BLOCKING BLITZES

The White Series is relatively safe from shooting backers. In plays 38-X and 39-Pitch the shooting backer is coming to the offensive halfback who is assigned to block him. In 47-Drive alternate blocking is used (Figure 4-37).

The hard-charging backer is very easily blocked by the off guard who, in alternate blocking, is blocking outside.

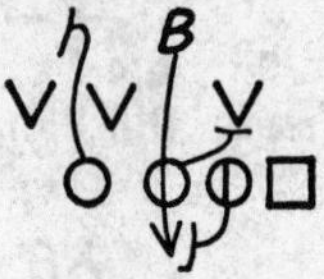

Figure 4-37
White 47-Drive with Alternate Blocking

The Multiple-Use Blue Series

The Blue Series, which is the final series in the Tight-Slot attack, is one that has several tactical uses. It has but four running plays and is always taught in slot-right and slot-left formations. This brings about a whipsaw action against the defense, which is not always equally adept at defending both sides. Once the "soft" side is determined, the Blue Series is able to pound that area.

A SHORT YARDAGE AND GOAL-LINE ATTACK

In these instances we are not looking for long yardage but, rather, almost certain short gains. Because in short yardage and goal-line situations the defense, by necessity, is coming hard to stop relatively short gains, we rarely see blitzes, stunts, loops, or slants. What we do see are special defenses to stop short gains. Therefore, we teach the Blue Series against the 6-5, the Gap-8, and the Tight 5-2 defenses.

FROM INSIDE-OUT TO OUTSIDE-IN

You have already seen how the Red Series and White Series are both oriented around first attacking the inside. Then, when the defense is drawn in, the attack is moved to the corner where there exists greater probability for longer gains. The Blue Series works from outside in. We begin by attacking the corners first and, if needed, work back inside or counter.

USE OF POWER BLOCKING

Finally, the Blue Series uses power blocking at the point of attack. In each instance, at least three offensive players are pitted against two defenders on the line of scrimmage, and other players lead or sift through into the secondary.

BLUE 41–POWER

The leadoff play is 41-Power. This is a strong off-tackle play which double-team blocks to the inside, kicks out at the corner, and runs two lead blockers ahead of the ball carrier (Figures 5-1, 5-2, 5-3).

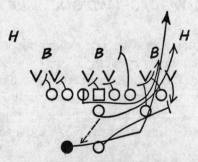

Figure 5-1
Blue 41-Power Versus 6-5 Defense

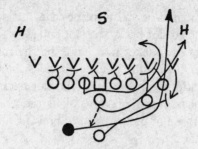

Figure 5-2
Blue 41-Power Versus Gap-8 Defense

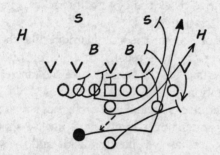

Figure 5-3
Blue 41-Power Versus 5-2 Tight Defense

BASE BLOCKING RULES

S.E. Inside; seal
S.B. On; inside
S.T. Inside; on; backer
S.G. Inside; on; backer
C. On; away
O.G. Lead
O.T. Fill
O.E. Fill

Position Play

The slot end drives down on the first man over his slot back.
He and the slot back are joined in a post-and-drive blocking com-

bination in which the slot end furnishes the outside power. But, if no defender is on the slot back, the slot end seals the inside of the hole and prevents the backer from entering the running lane.

If a defender is on him, the slot back is the post in a drive-and-post combination with his end. The slot back drives into the defender's belt buckle and prevents penetration. He must then close his hips to those of the slot and to prevent the defender from splitting them apart.

The slot tackle posts any man on him, reverse shoulder blocks any man immediately inside, and, if none of these exists, sifts through the line to block the closest linebacker. His primary job is to prevent penetration.

The rules of play for the slot guard are like those for the slot tackle. However, he will usually find his opponent inside; the closest on player may be the backer. Like the tackle, he, too, must prevent penetration.

The center blocks on and away. He uses a near shoulder block to block an opponent over him, and a reverse shoulder block to handle an opponent away. Like the tackle and the guard, he must also prevent penetration.

The off guard is a lead blocker. He pulls an arc across the line of scrimmage, cuts up into the hole area and uses a running shoulder block on the first opponent he sees.

The off tackle and the off end fill the area to their inside. They must deny penetration and use a high-bridge cross-body block to get this done.

Aiming at a spot one yard behind his slot end, the fullback drives out on the first defender showing at the corner. He will not have time to maneuver. He aims his forehead at the opponent's numbers and drives toward the sideline. If that defender is coming tight, the fullback will drive his inside shoulder into the front leg of the defender and, with this chop block, knock him down. The ball carrier will then adjust to the outside course.

Reversing to the slot side, the quarterback tosses the ball to the running back, and then continues on as a lead blocker. Like the off guard, he will use a running shoulder block on the first defender he sees.

The halfback catches the toss and immediately looks for the block at the corner. He drives into the opening and uses the blocks by the off guard and the quarterback to continue forward.

Coaching Points

We stress that this is a power play—nothing fancy about it. We are driving the defensive tackle from his area, kicking out the corner, and cutting off the pursuit of the backers. Furthermore, we are running two lead blockers ahead of the ball carrier. Only the fullback has to make an instant decision; if he finds the corner defender coming in tight and hard, he must knock him down. To do this, he aims his inside shoulder at the outside thigh of the defender and drives through the target. This chop block will almost always knock the defender down. Then the lead blockers will continue outside to escort the runner. The ball carrier must drive for yards, then feet, and finally inches!!!

BLUE 40-POWER

Blue 40-Power is the next play in this series and is used when we find the corner defender consistently coming hard and tight, and the perimeter being defended by a player from the secondary. Here we want to get to the corner quickly and run around him (Figures 5-4, 5-5, 5-6).

BASE BLOCKING RULES

S.E. Inside; seal
S.B. Corner
S.T. Inside; on; backer
S.G. Inside; on; backer
C. On; away
O.G. Lead
O.T. Fill
O.E. Fill

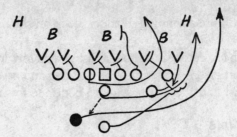

Figure 5-4
Blue 40-Power Versus 6-5 Defense

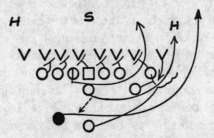

Figure 5-5
Blue 40-Power Versus Gap 8 Defense

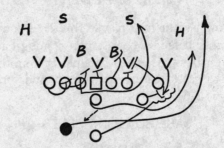

Figure 5-6
Blue 40-Power Versus 5-2 Tight Defense

Position Play

The slot end blocks down on the first defender inside. He must get his head across the crotch of that defender and hit with his outside shoulder. He must prevent penetration.

Responsible for the block at the corner, the slot back drives directly at that defender as fast as he can get there. He stays low and aims his shoulder at the outside thigh of the defender and drives straight through his leg. If this does not knock him down, the slot back slips into a cross-body block, maintains a high bridge, and crabs against the defender's legs.

As in 41-Power, the slot tackle posts any man on him, uses a reverse shoulder block on any man inside him, and, if none of these are present, sifts through the line and blocks the closest backer.

The slot guard acts exactly as does the slot tackle: inside; on; backer. He uses the same techniques as well.

The center blocks an on defender with a near shoulder block, and an away opponent with a reverse shoulder block. He must prevent penetration.

The off guard is the lead blocker. He pulls, gets depth, cuts up around the corner block, and then uses a running shoulder block on the first defender he sees.

The off tackle and off end fill inside and use a high cross-body block to prevent penetration.

The fullback is the cleanup blocker at the corner. He gets there with all possible speed, and is prepared to lend help to the slot back in knocking down the corner defender. If no help is needed, he continues upfield as a lead blocker.

Also a lead blocker is the quarterback. After reversing and tossing the ball to the halfback, he sprints on around the corner and uses a driving shoulder block on the first defender he sees.

Having caught the quarterback's toss, the halfback turns on all speed to get to the corner as quickly as he can. Once there, he reacts to the blocking and moves upfield.

Coaching Points

Once again we are stressing power and speed. All is exactly as in 41-Power, except that we are dealing with the corner defender in a different manner. In 41-Power, we gave him time to get depth so that we could kick him out. In 40-Power, we are denying depth so that we can shorten the corner, and get around him quickly. To do this, the slot back must get there fast and get him down. It is most important that the lead blockers keep as close together as possible, and furnish a moving wall behind which the ball carrier may run.

BLUE 44–TRAP

Having experienced 41-Power and 40-Power, many defensive units tend to fight very strongly in the direction of our backfield flow. When they are convinced of this trend to hitting the corner, they often become vulnerable to plays that hit behind the perceived thrust. In other words, the blocking scheme seems headed at the flank, but the actual path of the ball carrier is more inside. Such a play is Blue 44-Trap (Figures 5-7, 5-8, 5-9).

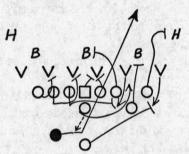

Figure 5-7
Blue 44-Trap Versus 6-5 Defense

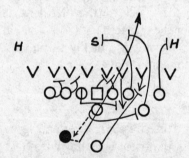

Figure 5-8
Blue 44-Trap Versus Gap-8 Defense

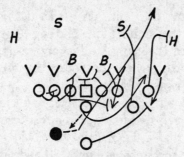

Figure 5-9
Blue 44-Trap Versus 5-2 Tight Defense

BASE BLOCKING RULES

S.E. Seal inside
S.B. Seal outside
S.T. Backer
S.G. Inside
 C. Slotside; on
O.G. Inside; backer
S.T. Trapper
S.E. Fill

Position Play

The slot end seals the inside edge of the running lane. He gets there quickly and uses a running, driving shoulder block to drive any opponent away.

Jab-stepping to allow his end to cross, the slot back moves forward to seal the outside edge of the running lane. He uses a running shoulder block to keep the area clear.

The slot tackle is responsible for the closest backer. He must get to him quickly and use a running shoulder block to furnish the needed drive. He must keep him from the path of the ball carrier.

The slot guard blocks inside. In all cases he will be working with his center in a double-team block.

The center blocks slot side; on. He is always working with his slot guard. Together they must drive that defender as far back as possible to widen the running lane and impede pursuit.

The off guard is responsible for any on-line defender to his inside. If there is no one there, he blocks the closest backer. In both cases he uses a cross-body block.

The trapper is the off tackle. He pulls close to the line of scrimmage and is prepared to block the first defender showing beyond the slot-guard area. He must use a shoulder block, keep good balance, and drive that opponent out. If that defender is scrambling on his hands and knees, the off tackle must drop to his own knees, smother the defender, and roll him out with vigorous leg and thigh action.

The off end pulls deep inside and, using a cross-body block, fills the area by blocking any opponent inside him.

The fullback drives at the first opponent on, or outside, the slot end and, using his outside shoulder, blocks that defender away from the hit area.

Reversing and tossing, the quarterback sprints wide around the defensive corner exactly as though running 40-Power.

The halfback catches the ball on his first step, takes a second step toward the sidelines, and then cuts up into the line of scrimmage behind the block of his off tackle.

Coaching Points

This play, to enjoy full success, must look exactly like a hit at the corner in its inception. As the halfback catches the ball, he must be facing the sideline, and he must continue so to face in his next step. In addition, the quarterback and fullback must go all out at the corner. It is the pull of the apparent sweep that makes this hit behind the pull successful.

BLUE 26–TRAP

After continuous pressure to the slot side, the defenders across from our slot side sometimes become careless in protecting their own territories, and become too eager to support the slot-side defenders. When this becomes evident, we strike the off-side defenders by first feinting to the slot side, and then coming back to the off side with Blue 26-Trap (Figures 5-10, 5-11, 5-12).

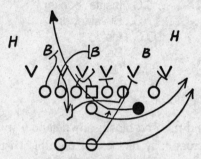

Figure 5-10
Blue 26-Trap Versus 6-5 Defense

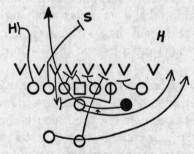

Figure 5-11
Blue 26-Trap Versus Gap-8 Defense

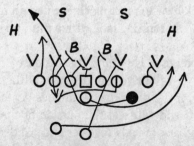

Figure 5-12
Blue 26-Trap Versus 5-2 Tight Defense

BLOCKING RULES

S.E. Fill
S.T. Trapper
S.G. Inside; backer
  C. Slotside; on
O.G. Inside
O.T. Backer
O.E. Seal

Position Play

The slot end fills and blocks any defender inside his position. He will use a cross-body block and prohibit that opponent from penetrating inside.

The slot tackle is the trapper. He pulls to the off side close to his line of scrimmage, and blocks out on the first defender showing beyond his off guard. If that defender is scrambling on his hands and knees, the slot tackle will drop to his own knees, smother the defender, and, using vigorous leg and thigh action, roll him out of the hole.

The slot guard blocks inside, then backer. It is his job to prevent any penetration across the line of scrimmage.

Blocking slot side, then on, the center is combining with his off guard to drive the defender in that area straight back.

With the center, the off guard is doubling to drive the common opponent back. Together they pinch him between their shoulders and ride him out of there.

The off tackle, who must block the defending linebacker, will seal the inside of the running lane with a running shoulder block on that backer.

The off end, too, is sealing the inside of the running lane. Like the tackle, he will drive that defender with a running shoulder block. However, if the defensive team does not have a defender in that area, the off end will seal the outside of the running lane.

The quarterback quickly reverses and hands the ball up to the slot back, who is approaching at full speed. He then continues to swing wide as in 40 or 41-Power.

The fullback must drive very fast into the line of scrimmage to block the first defender over, or outside the slot guard. He must beat the slot back.

Faking reception of the toss, the halfback sprints wide around the slot-side end exactly as in 40 and 41-Power.

Taking the handoff, the slot back looks for the block of his slot tackle. Then he cuts into the hole and flies upfield.

Coaching Points

To ensure success, this play must be run at high speed. There can be no hesitation or delay on the part of anyone. The fullback must get into the line of scrimmage without delaying the running of the slot back. Moreover, he must clear ahead of the quarterback. This action screens the ball carrier, and makes it very difficult for the defense to spot him in time, and the ball carrier, once through the hole, must make a short veer to the side and then head for the goal. This will get him away from the pursuit and isolate the deep-side defender.

6

The Tight-Slot Passing Game

Three separate, but related, segments combine to make up the Tight-Slot passing game. These are: play-action passes; drop-back passes; and screens, draws and statues.

Like our running game, our passing game has specific terminology that helps simplify the learning process.

GLOSSARY OF TERMS

Break: Pass route parallel to, but away from, the line of scrimmage towards the sideline.

Cross: A route crossing the field at a 45-degree angle.

Drag: Pass route parallel to the line of scrimmage.

Flag: Pass route starting upfield and then breaking at a 45-degree angle toward the corner of the playing field.

Hinge: Pass-protection method of blocking used in play-action passes in which the blocker first steps toward the play side, then pivots on that foot and opens to the other side to block a defender rushing the passer.

Slant: A route in which a detached receiver sprints quickly back towards the line of scrimmage at a tight angle.

Off Safety: The safety in a four-deep defense, who is aligned in front of our off side. Also called free safety.

Post: Pass route in which the receiver heads upfield and then cuts at 45 degrees toward the goal posts.

Slot Safety: The deep safety in a four-deep defense aligned on the side of our slot back. Also known as strong safety.

Swing: Pass route in which a player from the backfield runs wide around the corner.

Wall: A method of blocking in which all uncovered linemen release to the play side, turn back inside, and form a picket line behind which the ball carrier can run.

THEORY OF PLAY-ACTION PASSING

One of the difficulties in the passing game at the purely amateur level is the lack of time to put together a comprehensive, all-encompassing attack. Another is finding passers and receivers who can work together over a period of years—and, of course, gifted passers and receivers are very scarce.

From the defensive standpoint many coaches feel that the easiest thing to defend is the pass that is thrown in an obvious passing situation. On the other hand, many think that the most difficult task is to defend against passes that are thrown in a normal running situation. The Tight-Slot adheres to these beliefs, and so stresses first faking the run and then throwing the pass.

THEORY OF DROP-BACK PASSING

A large number of coaches believe that the drop-back pass, which gives an excellent view of the field, is a major weapon in the overall attack. This belief is undoubtedly valid when a truly good passer is combined with fine receivers. Even then, however, there are some factors present that tend to militate against the obvious pass.

In that situation, the defensive team is expecting a pass and the offense has lost the element of surprise. Accordingly, the defense is able to assume a specific posture suited entirely to foiling the awaited pass. This tends to burden the obvious pass with at least four probable results—not all of which are satisfactory.

The first, and most hoped for, is the completion of the pass for gain. Another is an incompletion resulting from an inaccurate throw or a dropped ball with the loss of down and no gain. The quarterback may be sacked with consequent loss of down and yardage, and the possibility of a fumble and loss of ball. Finally—and most unwelcome—the pass may be intercepted, which brings certain loss of the ball, loss of field position, and a possible score.

To somewhat offset this unfavorable 3-to-1 negative ratio, the Tight-Slot attack has refined its drop-back passing game.

First of all, we work very hard to insure completions by running routes that are within reach of our passer, within reasonable time limits, and relatively "safe." Safe routes are those that, by design, place the receiver between the ball and the defender, and so make it difficult to intercept. A lot of work is spent to prevent the sack by linemen and shooting backers, and constant effort is expended to upgrade the abilities of the passers and receivers. Most important, from our point of view, we do not throw a great variety of passes, but, rather, throw relatively few and work very hard to make them effective.

TECHNIQUE OF PASSING

If the quarterback does not set up correctly and throw properly, the passing attack has little chance for success. Accordingly, the quarterback sets up under the center with his hands placed so that the ball, when snapped, will arrive with the laces across the fingers of the passing hand. Pushing off his foot opposite his throwing arm, and making a quarter turn to the outside, he retreats with all possible speed to a depth of about 7 yards. He then braces on the foot that corresponds to his arm used in throwing. The ball is held at shoulder height with both hands, and gripped with two or three fingers on the laces. His index finger points toward the rear of the ball, and there is absolutely no palm pressure. When he is ready to throw, the ball is raised to his ear, and held at an angle of 45 degrees to the line of flight. His elbow is pointed down, and his other arm is extended to assist in balance. Now he steps forward in the pocket and crisply releases the ball by stepping over his front foot, which is pointed directly at the target. Having released the ball, the quarterback now puts himself in a position to help in the event of an interception. Length, lead, and zip are acquired by constant practice.

TECHNIQUE OF RECEIVING

Just as the quarterback must learn to set and throw correctly, so must the receivers be able to catch the ball.

The single most important technique is that the ball is always caught in the hands, and hands and arms must be relaxed.

A ball arriving at chest height or higher is caught with the hands cupped and the thumbs touching each other. The ball is always caught in the fingers and never in the palms of the hands.

If the ball is caught below chest height, the hands are again cupped but, now, the little fingers are touching.

When the ball is approaching away to the side, the little fingers are again touching, and the palms are facing toward the line of flight. Again the fingers control the reception.

On lead passes, the receiver must keep on running to get under the ball. He must not leap or jump. Forward progress cannot be made while he is in the air.

PLAY-ACTION PASS PROTECTION

The play-action pass must, in the initial stage, resemble a running play. The Tight-Slot uses its 1 play blocking system to give

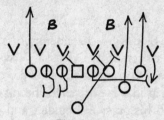

Figure 6-1
Red or Blue Pass Protection Versus Even Defense

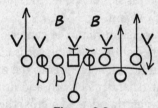

Figure 6-2
Red or Blue Pass Protection Versus Odd Defense

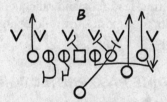

Figure 6-3
Red or Blue Pass Protection Versus Gap Defense

that early impression when throwing from the Red or Blue Series actions (Figures 6-1, 6-2, 6-3).

BLOCKING RULES

S.T. On; inside
S.G. Corner
C. On; away
O.G. Hinge
O.T. Hinge
F.B. Fill

Position Play

The slot tackle blocks any defender on him. He drives into his numbers and raises to screen the defender's vision. He must not allow any penetration. If there is no defender on him, the tackle blocks the first man inside. He drives his head beyond that defender's crotch, hits with his outside shoulder, and keeps the defender on the line of scrimmage.

The slot guard pulls to the corner and blocks out on the first defender on or beyond his slot end. He, too, hits in the numbers to screen the opponent's vision.

If there is a defender on him, the center drives into his numbers and prevents penetration. If no player is across from him, the center blocks away on the first defender to the off side. He must get his head beyond that defender's crotch and drive with his outside shoulder. He must not let that defender cross the line of scrimmage.

The off guard and off tackle hinge block. In executing this block they both, staying low, take a lead step toward the slot side. Now they pivot on that lead foot and quickly open up toward the off side. They are in good position to block any defender chasing the play from behind.

WHITE PASS PROTECTION

Just as Red and Blue play-action pass protection simulates 1-hole blocking, so does White protection resemble the 7 blocking scheme (Figures 6-4, 6-5, 6-6).

BLOCKING RULES

S.B. Corner
S.T. On; outside
S.G. On; fill
C. On; fill
O.G. On; fill
O.T. On; outside

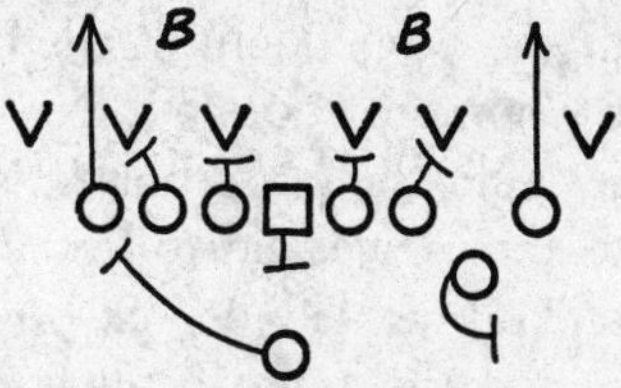

Figure 6-4
White Pass Protection Versus Even Defense

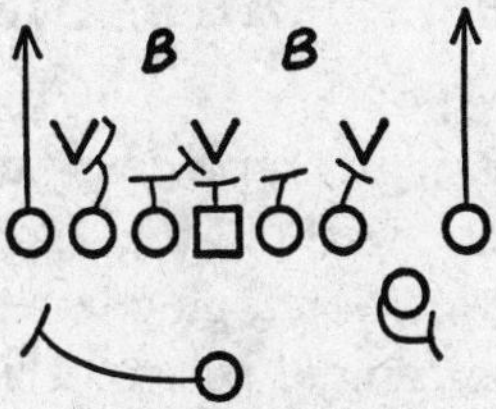

Figure 6-5
White Pass Protection Versus Odd Defense

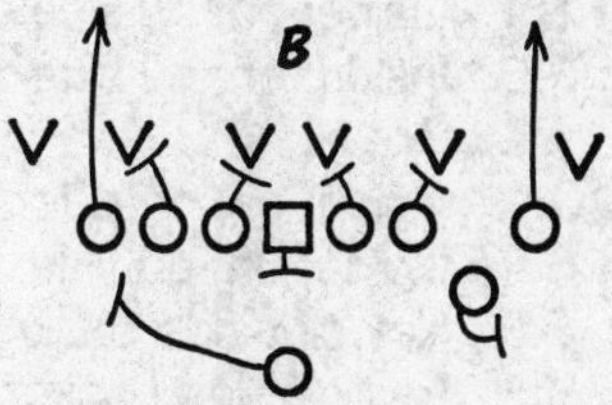

Figure 6-6
White Pass Protection Versus Gap Defense

Position Play

The slot tackle, using his outside shoulder, drives any player opposite him toward the sideline. He must keep that player from chasing the passer from behind. He forces the defender to take an outside course. If no player opposes him, the tackle will attack the first defender outside. He drop steps with his outside foot, and then blocks with his outside shoulder. Again, he must not let that player cross to his inside.

The slot guard, if an opponent is on him, drives into his numbers, screens his vision, and does not let that player penetrate. If no defender opposes him, the guard holds his position to prevent blitzes or, in their absence, gives aid to his center.

The off guard and off tackle block exactly as in base blocking for a 7 play. They open the hole to allow the halfback to get through to run his course.

DROP-BACK PASS PROTECTION

Protecting the passer in an obvious passing situation is more difficult but nonetheless vital to the success of the pass. The Tight-Slot scheme provides for coping with the rush of the defensive linemen and the blitzing of backers (Figures 6-7, 6-8, 6-9).

BLOCKING RULES

S.T. Inside; on; outside
S.G. Inside; on; outside
C. On; fill
O.G. Inside; on; outside
O.T. Inside; on; outside
S.B. Key slot-side backer
F.B. Key off-side backer
H.B. Key off-side end

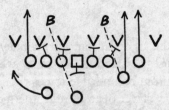

Figure 6-7
Drop-Back Pass Protection Versus Even Defense

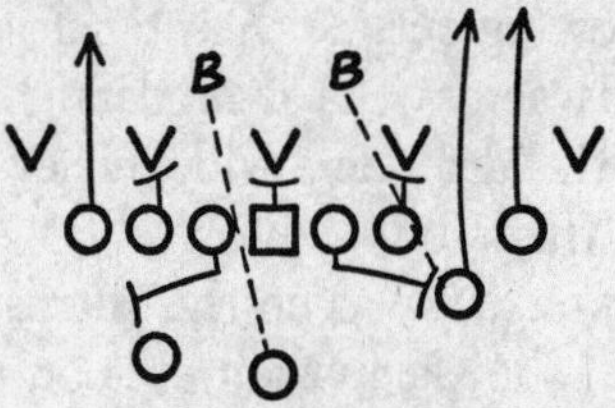

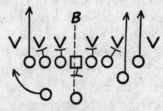

Figure 6-8
Drop-Back Pass Protection Versus Odd Defense

Figure 6-9
Drop-Back Pass Protection Versus Gap Defense

Position Play

The guards, if covered, concentrate on the belt buckles of the defensive linemen across from them. They set up inside and force the defenders outside. They must never let them get inside because that is the shortest way to the ball. They drive into the defenders' numbers and bring their arms and shoulders up to keep the opponents away from their jerseys and shoulder pads. Constantly keeping their legs pumping, they retreat over and over again. They must keep their heads in front of the defenders. If the defenders charge to the outside, the guards use their inside shoulders to force the opponents away from the pocket; if the defenders charge inside, the guards use their outside shoulders to drive those defenders down the line. If the defenders come straight ahead with force the guards—after firing into their numbers—throw heads and shoulders across tne defenders to cut their feet from under them. When the guards have no opponent playing over them, they drop and prepare to play the first defender showing outside their tackles. In doing this, they must get their heads across the defenders, hit with their inside shoulders, and run the defenders wide. They must never let the defenders get inside them.

The tackles play exactly as do the guards. When faced by an opponent over them, they keep their eyes on the belt buckles, set up inside and force the defenders outside. They, too, keep their feet chopping, and hit, hit, retreat, and hit again. If the defenders take an inside course, the tackles drive their heads across their crotches, hit with their outside shoulders and drive the defenders down.

The center, if covered, braces and eyes the belt buckle of the defender. If that defender goes to either side, the center drives his head across the defender's crotch and keeps him going. However, if that opponent is coming hard at him, the center, after stopping his charge and initial thrust, cuts the defender's legs away by throwing a cross-body block and maintaining a high bridge.

The slot back (and quarterback) first key the slot-side line backer. If that backer is blitzing, the slot back is ready at once to catch the ball as the quarterback, reading the blitz, quickly flips the ball to the area vacated by that linebacker.

The fullback is responsible for any blitz by the off-side line backer. If that backer is coming, the fullback steps up and takes him on, and the play goes as planned. However, if that backer is not coming, the fullback swings wide and becomes a possible outlet. This check-release by the fullback can be controlled by the quarterback. Normally, the fullback swings to the side of the flow. But, if the quarterback thinks the defensive is reacting to that swing, he can have the fullback swing the other way by simply adding "opposite" to the play call, and the fullback will swing to the other side.

The halfback, too, makes a check-release. If he sees a long line, 6 or 7, he will block the end man if he comes. However, if that player is not coming at once, the halfback will continue his course.

7

Tight-Slot Play-Action Passing

There are seven basic passes in this group of play-action passes. Three of them are thrown from the Red Series look; two from the White Series look; and two from the look of the Blue Series. All of these passes first feint a run, and then end in a pass.

RED 41–PASS

The 41-Pass (Figures 7-1, 7-2) is the first in the basic Red play-action passes. In the beginning it looks like 41-Square, and is used when the defense has become crowded toward the line of scrimmage in order to stop the run. The run look encourages the defensive secondary to react to a perceived off-tackle play, and this initial reaction by the defense allows our prime receiver to reach the reception area free to catch the ball.

Position Play

The interior linemen execute Red play-action pass protection as described in the previous chapter.

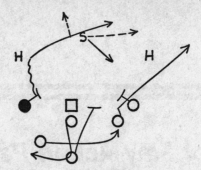

Figure 7-1
Red 41-Pass Versus 3-Deep Defense

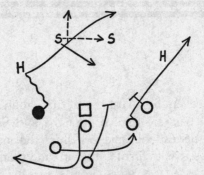

Figure 7-2
Red 41-Pass Versus 4-Deep Defense

The slot end blocks down exactly as in run 41-Square. He gets his helmet across the defender's crotch, hits with the outside shoulder, and prevents penetration.

Jab-stepping to allow the end to clear in front of him, the slot back then breaks at a 45-degree angle toward the sideline.

The off end, who is the prime receiver, slams the first defender inside. He then releases as though to block the wide deep defender. However, he is keying the middle deep defender when the defense is postured in 3-deep. Now, if that defender is filling toward the line of scrimmage, the off end continues his path. That will place him behind the defense and in excellent position to receive the ball. If that defender is moving in a lateral direction (dotted line), the off end turns directly upfield. This second break will again put the off end behind the defense. When the defense is in a 4-deep, the off end now keys the off safety, and reacts to his moves just as he did to those of the middle safety in the 3-deep.

The quarterback reverses out, hands the ball to the halfback and either rolls or chases. He does not fake pass.

Coaching Points

The slot end must make a good, hard block. He is convincing the deep defender on his side that a run is in progress. This may bring that defender up quickly toward the line of scrimmage. Now the slot back reacts to that player. If he is coming toward the line of scrimmage, the slot back will go on by him. However, if that defender is backtracking and playing pass, the slot back will at once make a 90-degree turn to his sideline. He is the second choice receiver.

Of great concern are the moves of the off end. He must not get to the reception area too quickly. He must give the defender he is keying time enough to start his reaction to the apparent run. Therefore, he must give a deliberate slam to the first inside defender. As he is doing this, he is watching his key. Then he must head directly at the wide deep defender, his side, before making his cut. By playing in this manner, he can be practically certain to get behind the defense in the deep middle area.

The acting of the passer is most important. He must look hard at the blocking at the corner just exactly as in running the off-tackle play. There is no need for him, at this time, to look for the off end—he knows where he will be. Then, as he approaches close to the corner, he now looks for the prime receiver in the middle area. If that off end is open, he throws to him. If he is not open, the halfback switches his vision to the area in which the slot back is running, and, if open, throws to him. If he cannot get to either of these receivers, he will throw over the sidelines beyond the slot back. BUT—if the halfback reaches the corner and finds running room there, he will seat the ball and RUN.

RED 33–PASS

The next basic play-action pass in the Red series is Red 33-Pass. When the slot-side linebacker is crowding the line of scrimmage, or coming up fast to meet our bucking fullback, we are ready to throw. The backer cannot be in close to stop the run and, at the same time, be back to defend against the pass (Figures 7-3, 7-4).

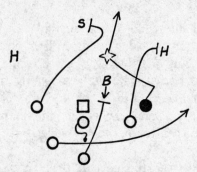

Figure 7-3
Red 33-Pass Versus 3-Deep Defense

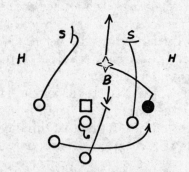

Figure 7-4
Red 33-Pass Versus 4-Deep Defense

Position Play

Regular Red play pass protection is employed from tackle to tackle.

The slot end is the designated receiver. He jab steps at a 45-degree angle to the outside to allow the slot back to clear inside, and to allow time for the slot-side backer to get moving toward the line of scrimmage. Then the slot end cuts upfield at a slight inside angle, and is prepared to catch the ball at a depth of not more than 4 yards. He then turns upfield to use the blockers ahead of him there.

Releasing immediately, the slot back goes directly at the wide deep defender in a 3-deep and applies a running shoulder block or a cross-body block. If the defense is 4-deep, the slot back blocks on the slot-side safety.

The off end streaks to, and blocks, the middle safety in a 3-deep defense and, if the defense is 4-deep, he blocks the off safety. He, too, uses a running shoulder or cross-body block.

The quarterback reverses, fakes the ball to the fullback, and then braces immediately to flip the ball to the slot end.

Meanwhile, the fullback has driven into the line just as though he has the ball, and hopes to collide with the slot-side backer. However, if that does not take place, the fullback veers to the off side and prepares to block the deep defender that side.

The halfback crosses to the corner and then looks back. He is an outlet if, for any reason, the quarterback has not been able to throw the ball.

Coaching Points

It is important that the slot end not get into the reception area too soon. He must allow the pull of the play to draw the backer in. Then, of course, it's too late, and the slot end will be beyond the backer's vision, and free to catch the ball. He cannot get too deep—four yards in depth assure that he will catch the ball before the slot back and off end apply their blocks. If they block before the ball is caught, the pass is illegal. He must be made to realize that the throw is not deep but, with assigned blockers ahead of him, a good opportunity exists for a very good gain. Nor can the quarterback rush the play. He must make a deliberate fake to the bucking

fullback. That will bring the backer into the line and away from the
receiving area.

RED 10–PASS

The final basic Red Series pass is Red 10-Pass. This is a bootleg
pass and is used when the defensive secondary is in fast rotation to
help stop an apparent run to the side of the slot back (Figures 7-5,
7-6).

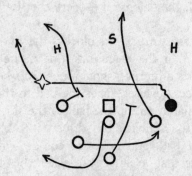

Figure 7-5
Red 1-Pass Versus 3-Deep Defense

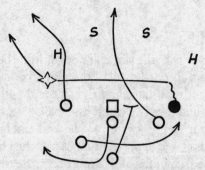

Figure 7-6
Red 10-Pass Versus 4-Deep Defense

Position Play

All the interior linemen use regular 9 blocking. In other words, they block exactly as though the play were a running reverse. In this case, the quarterback, in the huddle, gives both the play call and blocking designation.

The slot end jab steps at a 45-degree angle to let the slot back clear and to delay his own takeoff. Then, as the secondary is getting into movement, he proceeds upfield 4 or 5 yards at the wide deep receiver or, in 4-deep, at the slot safety. Now, he cuts inside and runs a drag route across the line of scrimmage. He will get the ball in the area just outside the original position of the off end.

Taking off at once, the slot back, if confronted by a 3-deep, runs through the area of the middle safety. If the defense is in a 4-deep, the slot back splits the distance between the two safeties.

First slamming the first defender inside, the off end releases at the outside shoulder of the deep wide defender, and keeps on that course until the ball is thrown. Then he will curl back inside and see if he cannot block for the slot end who, by this time, is in possession of the ball.

The fullback drives into the slot-side line as in all Red plays. If he is not tackled, he will break flat to the slot side to draw some defender with him.

Continuing straight across, the halfback fakes an off-tackle run.

The quarterback reverses out and makes a very deliberate fake to the crossing halfback. Then, with the ball behind his back thigh, he continues to roll toward the off side, and releases the ball to the slot end coming across on his drag route.

Coaching Points

Once again, the slot end must let the slot back clear first. This helps the timing of the play because it stops that end from arriving in the reception area too soon.

Likewise, the quarterback cannot rush the play. He must proceed exactly as in 41-Square. He makes a good fake and, placing the ball behind his back thigh, continues to roll toward the off side as though he had nothing in particular in mind. He does not look upfield at once. He wants that wide deep defender on the off side to keep moving toward the slot side. Now, when the slot end appears in the reception area, the ball is thrown. If the quarterback is rolling to his left, he must use a special technique in order to throw with accuracy. When he is ready to release the ball, the quarterback plants with his left foot, brings his right foot behind his left, steps out with his left and throws.

WHITE 47–PASS

The next group in our basic play-action passes belongs to the White Series. There are two passes in this series and all, at the start, look like the running action of the White Series. The first play in this set is 47-Pass. It is designed to look like a busted 47 run, and is used when the defensive secondary is playing close to stop the running game (Figures 7-7, 7-8).

Position Play

The interior linemen and the slot back employ regular White drop-back pass protection.

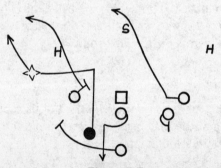

Figure 7-7
White 47-Pass Versus 3-Deep Defense

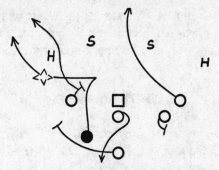

Figure 7-8
White 47-Pass Versus 4-Deep Defense

The slot end releases at the deep middle man in a 3-deep defense; if the defense is 4-deep, he releases at the off safety. In both cases, after the ball is thrown, he will peel back and block that defender.

Slamming the first man inside, the off end sprints through the position of the wide safety on the off side, and, after the throw he, too, peels back to block that defender.

Swinging to the off side, the fullback blocks on the corner defender. He drives his helmet into that defender's numbers, and keeps erect to block his vision.

The halfback drives through the line, gets upfield 4 or 5 yards and then breaks at a 90-degree angle toward the sidelines. Now he catches the ball, adjusts to his blockers, and heads for the goal.

As he reverses out, the quarterback fakes to the halfback, drops back to his pocket, and flips the ball to the halfback in his break pattern.

Coaching Points

It is very important that the quarterback and halfback make a poor fake during the handoff. This allows the off-side backer to see that the halfback does not have the ball. Accordingly, there is no reason for the backer to tackle him, and this lets him get freely into his pass pattern. The halfback, upon reaching his depth, will casually look inside and then cut suddenly outside on his break pattern.

He is creating the illusion that something has gone wrong with the play—a busted play. All of this tends to get defensive attention away from him and enhance his chances of arriving at the reception area free and clear.

WHITE 30–PASS

White 30-Pass is the final pass in the White Series. It, too, looks like 47-Drive and is used when the off-side backer is busily engaged in stopping that run (Figures 7-9, 7-10).

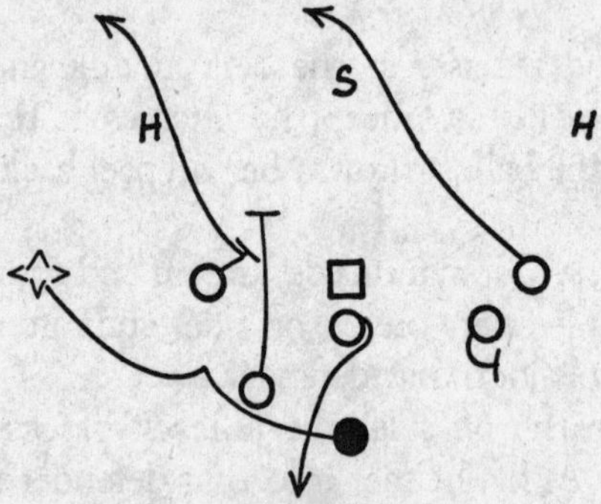

Figure 7-9
White 30-Pass Versus 3-Deep Defense

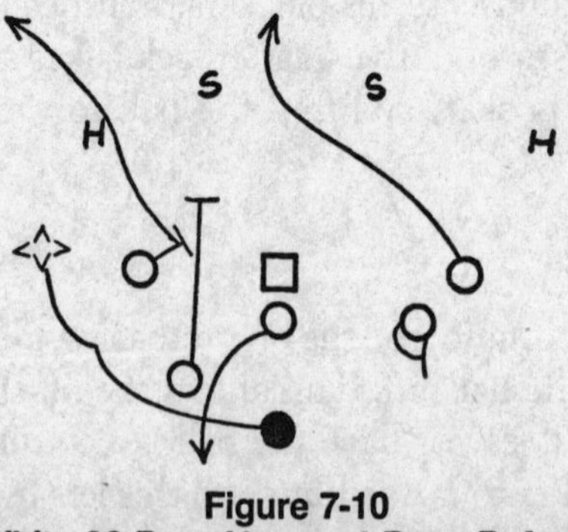

Figure 7-10
White 30-Pass Versus 4-Deep Defense

Position Play

From tackle to tackle, and including the slot back, White play-action pass protection is used.

Just as in White 47-Pass, the slot end sprints through the position of a middle 3-deep defender, or that of the off-side safety in a 4-deep. Again he will peel back to block after the ball is thrown.

Likewise, the off end—after his slam—will run through the area off the wide deep off-side defender, and will also peel back to block after the throw.

The halfback runs a very hard fake drive play and tries to collide with the backer. Failing in that, he breaks at once toward the slot sideline.

The fullback fakes at the corner defender, slips him and swings wide ready to catch the ball.

Reversing out, the quarterback makes a very deliberate, good fake to the driving halfback, sets up and then releases the ball to the fullback.

Coaching Points

Here we must have an excellent fake between the quarterback and the halfback. Such a fake will ensure that the backer will stay home. We want him there—not chasing the fullback in the flat— and, if at all possible, the halfback must collide with that backer. Now, as the fullback approaches the corner defender, he must hit him lightly with his inside shoulder and forearm. Then he slips off outside and at once looks for the ball. That should arrive at just about the extension of the line of scrimmage.

BLUE 40–PASS

Our last two basic play-action passes are run from the fake of the Blue series action. These two passes are run first—pass second—oriented. Both are thrown from the run action that attacks the corner. The first of these two passes is Blue 40-Pass, and

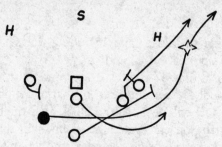

Figure 7-11
Blue 40-Pass Versus 3-Deep Defense

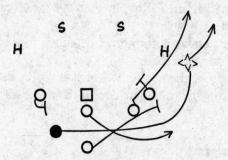

Figure 7-12
Blue 40-Pass Versus 4-Deep Defense

this is thrown when the slot side of the defense is coming fast and hard to stop the run (Figures 7-11, 7-12).

Position Play

The interior line and the slot end execute Blue play-action pass protection, which is exactly like that of Red play action.

The slot back jab steps to allow the slot end to clear and then sprints upfield outside a 3-deep wide defender, and outside the slot safety if the defense is 4-deep.

The fullback gets quickly to the corner and blocks on the first defender he finds there. If that defender is coming deep, the fullback, using his outside shoulder, will drive that player toward the sideline. If that player is coming tight, the fullback will hit him with his inside shoulder on the thigh and knock him off his feet.

The halfback sprints across the line of scrimmage around the corner defender and looks for the ball. He is the prime receiver.

The quarterback rolls out to the slot side, fakes a toss to the halfback, and drives at the off-tackle hole. If that area is clear, he will keep the ball and run. If there is no clear running room, he will throw the ball forward to the halfback.

Coaching Points

The slot end must make a hard and aggressive block. He must convince the defense that the play is a run.

By the same token, the fullback must out-block the corner defender or get him down. Furthermore, the quarterback and halfback must act correctly. As the quarterback fakes his toss, the halfback extends his arms and hands as though preparing to catch the ball and then swing wide as in a sweep.

The quarterback has the ball hidden behind his back thigh as he is approaching the corner. He must be moving forward as he makes his decision. If the hole is open, he will secure the ball and drive through; if not, he will release to the halfback, who is entering the area cleared out by the slot back.

BLUE 43-PASS

The second and last play in the Blue Series is Blue 43-Pass. This is a throw to the off end, who is slipping behind the middle safety in a 3-deep and the off safety in a 4-deep. This play is used when attention has drifted away from the off end who, in this Blue Series has not yet been downfield on plays to the slot side (Figures 7-13, 7-14).

Position Play

Blue play-action pass protection is used by the slot end and the interior linemen.

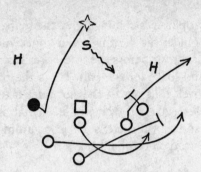

Figure 7-13
Blue 43-Pass Versus 3-Deep Defense

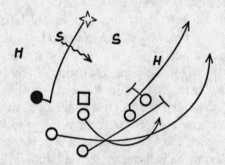

Figure 7-14
Blue 43-Pass Versus 4-Deep Defense

The slot back jab steps to allow the slot end to clear for his inside block. Then, if the defense is 3-deep, the slot back releases through the area of the wide deep defender. If the defense is 4-deep, the slot back runs through the area of the slot-side safety.

The fullback acts exactly as in the previous play. The halfback, too, will fake the sweep.

Now, the off end, who is the prime receiver, has been watching the middle deep defender in a 3-deep and the off safety in a 4-deep. He has taken an inside jab step and is keeping low. As soon as the defender moves away from this area, the off end sprints to, and in back of, that spot. It is there that he will catch the ball.

The quarterback does exactly as he did in Blue 40-Pass. Now, however, he will release the ball to the off end, who is behind the deep coverage.

Coaching Points

This is a game of cat and mouse between the off end and the defensive secondary. If the off end is too quick, he will be covered; if he is too late, we might not be able to throw. Accordingly, the off end must correctly study that defender whenever any slot-side Blue play is run. By so doing he will learn the time interval of that opponent in movement towards the slot side. With this information the off end can adjust his burst to arrive in the area of reception just enough behind that defender so that he cannot recover. Then the off end will be clear. The off wide deep defender cannot get to the ball without committing a foul.

8

Drop-Back Passing

The Tight-Slot passing game is made up of ten basic pass plays. Four of these are used against teams playing a 3-deep defense, and the remaining six versus opponents positioned in a 4-deep. All plays are effective against man-to-man or zone defenses. Regular or alternate blocking is used to protect the passer.

ROSE AND LIZ

When using the drop-back pass, the normally close formation is slightly modified. Both ends are split away four yards. This lets them escape from the line of scrimmage more easily, and still allows us to use our running game. In addition, all drop-back passes are used from both right and left formations (Figures 8-1, 8-2).

In moving to left formation (LIZ), only four players are switched. These receivers run the basic patterns from both sides. This simple switch doubles our passing look with almost no effort by us, but it greatly burdens the defense, who not only have to contend with additional patterns but also must cover different indi-

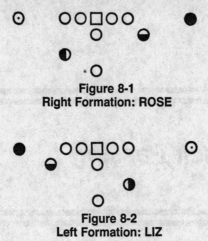

Figure 8-1
Right Formation: ROSE

Figure 8-2
Left Formation: LIZ

viduals with different running speeds and faking movements. In consequence, not any one defender can be used to covering the same back all the time, and this adds to his task.

ROSE 61–PASS

The first in the group of four 60-series passes, 61-Pass, divides the slot-side deep coverage and opens an area into which our off end can enter to catch the pass (Figure 8-3).

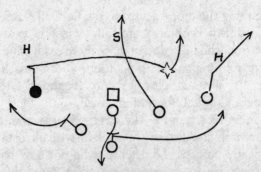

Figure 8-3
Rose 61-Pass Versus 3-Deep Man or Zone

Position Play

The slot end runs at the outside shoulder of the wide deep defender, his side, angles towards the flag, and takes that man with him.

Similarly, the slot back runs at the closest shoulder of the middle safety, veers toward the post, and brings the defender along.

The off end, who is the prime receiver, drives quickly at the wide deep defender, his side, cuts diagonally across the field, and makes the reception in the area between the original positions of the safety and halfback.

Using a check-release, the fullback swings to the slot side to draw the backer on that side away from the flight path of the ball.

The halfback checks the corner, his side, and blocks any rusher. None coming, he swings wide and becomes an outlet.

The quarterback drops quickly to his pocket, keeping his eye on the middle deep defender. If that player is in retreat, the quarterback knows he's home free to pass to the prime receiver. However, if the defender is moving in a lateral direction toward the slot side, the ball is released to the slot back in the middle area.

Coaching Points

The routes of the slot end and slot back must be run as drawn to insure that the area of reception will become enlarged. It doesn't matter whether the defense is man or zone; the safety and halfback must pick up our receivers and stay with them. Now, the off end uses fast foot and arm movement to help drive the defender on his side to retreat and then cuts quickly to the vacated area. He must not get deeper than seven yards, and should be receiving the ball in front of the space originally occupied by the slot back.

ROSE 62–PASS

The second pass in our attack against the 3-deep defense is Rose 62. This pattern brackets the middle deep defender and also threatens him short and deep simultaneously (Figure 8-4).

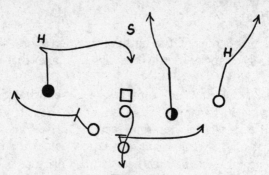

Figure 8-4
Rose 62-Pass Versus 3-Deep Man or Zone

Position Play

As in Rose 61, the slot end releases at the wide defender, his side, and takes him back and out.

The slot back also does exactly as he did in the former pass and runs to get deep behind the middle safety.

The fullback and halfback do exactly as before.

Now, however, the off end must adjust his timing to arrive in front of the middle safety just as the slot back is arriving behind him. Right now, instead of continuing across the field, he curls quickly back toward the line of scrimmage.

The quarterback drops into his pocket, looks to the middle of the field, and passes to whichever of those two receivers is open.

Coaching Points

This play looks a good deal like pass 61—and is so intended. The receivers must make the correct moves with the proper timing. This being so, we will have a receiver open. In addition, we are setting up the wide deep defenders for the last two plays in the series.

ROSE 63–PASS

The next pass in this group is Rose 63. This play is a breakout under the slot-side deep defender. Up to this point, we have been

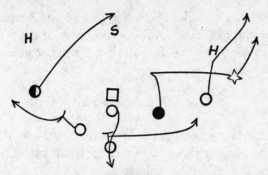

Figure 8-5
Rose 63-Pass Versus 3-Deep Man or Zone

taking this defender deep, and now it is time to throw in front of him (Figure 8-5).

Position Play

As in the previous two plays, the slot end continues to force the wide deep defender back and out.

Now, the slot back begins his route exactly as in passes 61 and 62. As he reaches a depth of about five yards, he suddenly breaks to the sideline at a 90-degree angle. He is the prime receiver.

In this play, the off end has only one thought. He races as fast as he can to get deep behind the area of the safety. He is the second-choice receiver.

The fullback and halfback do exactly as before.

The quarterback gets quickly into his pocket and looks for the slot back on his break pattern. If that player is free, he releases the ball to him. If not, he looks upfield to the off end, whose surprise move has probably placed him behind the safety.

Coaching Points

It is very important that the slot end and slot back make this play look exactly like the previous two. Now the defensive safety, if playing man-to-man, has no chance to get to our receiver. If they are in a zone, the wide deep defender is faced with a long-and-short situation which can be a no-win one. Finally, if the middle safety races up to assist the slot side, the off end will become open in the deep middle area.

ROSE 64–PASS

The last play against the 3-deep defense is Rose 64-Pass. This is a halfback swing to the off side and places our fastest back against coverage by the linebacker (Figure 8-6).

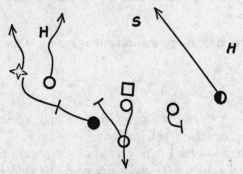

Figure 8-6
Rose 64-Pass Versus 3-Deep Man or Zone

Position Play

The slot end releases at the close shoulder of the middle deep defender and takes him deep upfield.

Both the fullback and slot back remain to furnish blocking and protect the passer.

Driving at the close shoulder of the wide deep defender, the off end makes a post cut to bring that defender along with him.

The halfback feints a block at the corner rusher, slips wide and swings upfield to make the catch.

Quickly dropping into his pocket, the quarterback looks deep and then transfers his attention to the halfback.

Coaching Points

The off end must do a good job and pull the wide deep defender back and away. He must give every indication that he is going to get the ball. The quarterback helps in this by looking hard at the off end until the last possible minute. Now the stage is set for our best back to outrun the backer, receive the ball, and take off goalward.

70 SERIES VERSUS 4-DEEP MAN OR ZONE

Like those in the 60 series, the passes in the 70 series are effective against the defense used. We run this series exclusively against 4-deep alignments, and the passes are adaptable to both man-to-man and zone defenses. Because teams very often switch their coverage from time to time, we must be ready to switch receivers, or routes, after the ball is snapped from center and the play is underway. To do this, we key one of the defenders and make our adjustments accordingly. That key, on plays aimed at the slot side, is the slot-side safety; on plays directed to the off side, the off-side safety. We always assume that the coverage is man-to-man until the key, by his actions, tell us it is not.

ROSE 71–PASS

The first pass in our attack against the deep defense is Rose 71. It clears out the wide deep defender on the slot side and frees the slot back in a breakout pattern (Figure 8-7).

Position Play

The slot end drives at the outside shoulder of the wide deep defender, angles toward the flag, and takes that defender deep.

Running hard at the slot safety, the slot back suddenly breaks out at a 90-degree angle and gets ready to catch the ball.

The halfback runs at the inside shoulder of the off safety and takes him deep.

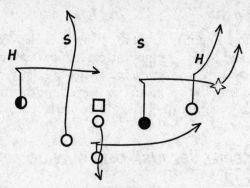

Figure 8-7
Rose 71-Pass Versus 4-Deep Man or Zone

First sprinting hard at the wide deep defender, his side, the off end now breaks at a 90-degree angle to his inside and runs a drag pattern across the line of scrimmage. He is the second-choice receiver.

The fullback check-releases and then swings to the slot side.

The quarterback drops into his pocket, checks the slot-side safety, and releases the ball.

Coaching Points

This is not a difficult read. If the slot safety is in quick pursuit of the slot back, the defense is man and that defender has a difficult job, because his angle of approach is bad. The slot back should be open. If the quarterback is in doubt, he will look back inside for the off end, who will be coming open over the middle. If that slot-side safety is in retreat, the quarterback reads zone and has free wheeling to the slot back. The check swing of the fullback has drawn the backer toward the sideline and kept him from his drop, but now again, the off end will be free as he drags across the middle.

ROSE 72–PASS

The second pass in this group is Rose 72. This is a drag route by the slot end in front of the area of the slot safety (Figure 8-8).

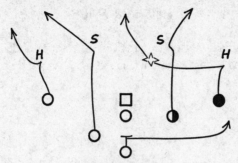

Figure 8-8
Rose 72-Pass Versus 4-Deep Man or Zone

Position Play

The slot end, who is the prime receiver, drives hard at the wide deep defender, his side. He executes a 90-degree break to the inside to run a drag route in front of the slot safety.

The slot back runs a deep course at the outside shoulder of the slot safety and takes him deep.

Both the off end and halfback run deep routes at their respective defenders.

The quarterback gets to his pocket, makes his read, and throws to the open receiver.

Coaching Points

Here we are bracketing the slot-side safety. Man or zone, he must go with the slot back. Now, if the defense is man-to-man, the wide deep defender has a difficult coverage on our dragging slot end, and that defender has no inside deep assistance. If they are playing zone, he is out of it altogether. The read for the quarterback is very simple. If the slot safety is up to cover the slot end crossing, our slot back is free and clear; if the safety goes deep, the slot end is open. The fullback check swing has removed the backer from the flight path.

ROSE 73–PASS

Rose 73-Pass is used to get the ball relatively deep to the slot end as he runs a post pattern (Figure 8-9).

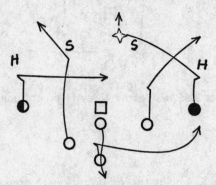

Figure 8-9
Rose 73-Pass Versus 4-Deep Man or Zone

Position Play

The slot end, the prime receiver, drives at the wide deep defender and then cuts for the post.

The slot back runs at his defender and breaks to the flag.

The halfback runs through the outside shoulder of the off safety and takes him away and outside.

First moving straight ahead, the off end then breaks at a 90-degree angle and runs a drag route over the middle parallel to the line of scrimmage. He is the secondary receiver.

The fullback checks and then releases to the slot side.

Coaching Points

The slot end, who is running a cross pattern will come open if the defense is playing man. He has his defender at a disadvantageous angle, and there will be no inside help because the halfback has pulled the off safety out of the reception area. If the defense is zone, that slot end will not be open as both deep defenders are in retreat on that side. However, it remains a simple read. The quarterback keys the slot safety and sees him retreating into zone coverage. That quarterback knows his slot end, too, will not be in the clear, but he also knows that the off end, who is running a drag route, will be coming open over the middle and acts accordingly.

ROSE 74–PASS

Rose 74-Pass is the next play in this group. It is a break route to our halfback coming underneath the deep coverage (Figure 8-10).

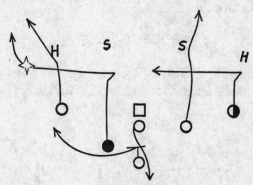

Figure 8-10
Rose 74-Pass Versus 4-Deep Man or Zone

Position Play

The off end drives at the outside shoulder of the wide deep defender, angles toward the flag, and draws that defender away.

Bursting hard and straight at the off safety, the halfback then breaks at a 90-degree angle toward the sideline. He is the prime receiver.

The slot back runs inside the slot safety to take him deep.

After a hard drive at the wide deep defender, the slot end breaks 90 degrees inside and runs a drag pattern across the line of scrimmage.

The fullback check-releases and then swings to the off side.

Dropping into his pocket, the quarterback reads his off safety key, and delivers the ball to the open man.

Coaching Points

The read is not involved. If the off safety is in fast pursuit of our halfback, that receiver will be free because the angle of pursuit puts that defender at a disadvantage. The check release pulls the backer out of the flight path. If, however, the off safety is in retreat, the defense is zone and the receiver is now more open. If the quarterback has any doubts, he is aware that the slot end is coming open over the middle.

ROSE 75–PASS

Next to last in this basic 70 series is Rose 75-Pass. This play is a drag route by the off end and brackets the off safety (Figure 8-11).

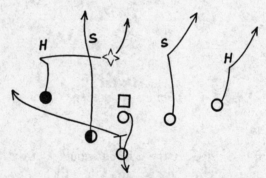

Figure 8-11
Rose 75-Pass Versus 4-Deep Man or Zone

Position Play

The prime receiver, the off end, drives at the wide deep defender to force him back. Now he cuts 90 degrees to the middle and runs a drag route in front of the off safety.

The halfback runs a deep course at the outside shoulder of the off safety and takes him deep.

Both the slot end and the slot back run deep patterns at their defenders.

Dropping into the pocket, the quarterback makes his read, and throws to the open receiver.

Coaching Points

The off-side safety is in a bind. Whatever the defense, he must cover the halfback. If the defense is man, the wide deep defender will have a most difficult time in covering our off end who, is running away from him to the inside. If the defense is in zone coverage, he's not even near. Our quarterback is reading the off safety. If that safety is coming up to cover the crossing off end, the halfback is home free; if the safety deepens, as in zone coverage, the off end is open.

ROSE 76–PASS

Rose 76-Pass is the last in this group of passes used against 4-deep coverage. This play frees the off end as he runs a route to the post (Figure 8-12).

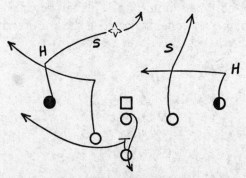

Figure 8-12
Rose 76-Pass Versus 4-Deep Man or Zone

Position Play

The off end is the prime receiver. He runs hard at the wide deep receiver, feints an out cut, and then goes for the post.

The halfback releases at the off safety and then breaks to the flag.

Running through the outside shoulder of the slot safety, the slot back pulls him away from the middle area.

The slot end moves straight forward and then runs a drag route across the line of scrimmage. He is the secondary receiver.

The fullback checks and swings to the off side.

Coaching Points

If the defense is playing man, the off end will come open. He is running a cross pattern with his halfback, who is drawing the off safety away from the post area. By the same token, the slot back is drawing the slot safety away. If the quarterback sees the off safety in quick retreat, he reads zone and at once knows that his prime receiver will not be open. He does know that the slot end, who is coming across the middle, will be free, and he will pass to him.

ALTERNATE BLOCKING

Just as our running game has alternate blocking schemes, so does our drop-back pass protection. This can be called in the huddle or, by calling out a code, indicated at the line of scrimmage after the team is over the ball (Figures 8-13, 8-14).

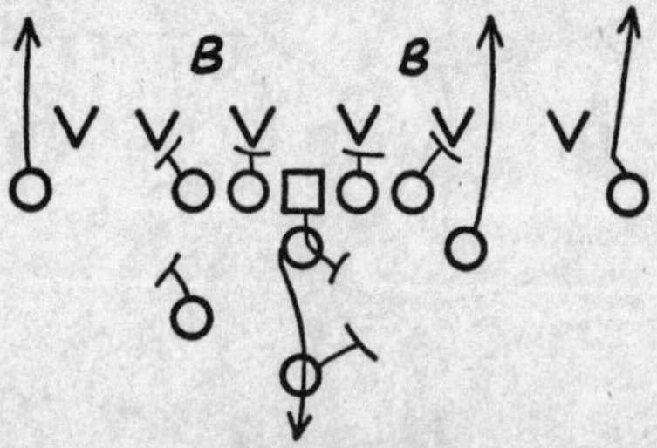

Figure 8-13
Alternate Drop-Back Protection Versus Even Defense

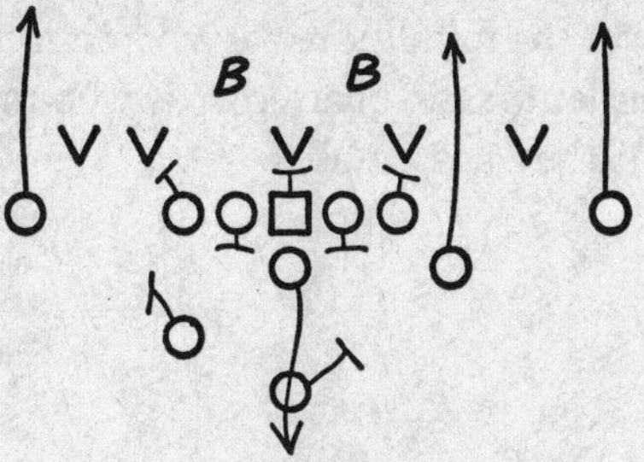

Figure 8-14
Alternate Drop-Back Protection Versus Odd Defense

BLOCKING RULES

Center. On; fill
Guards. On; fill
Tackles. On; outside
Backs. Check; release

Position Play

The center, using his regular technique, blocks any man on him. If there is no defender on him, the center steps back, looks left to right, and is prepared to give help where needed.

Both guards play opponents covering them on the line of scrimmage. If they are not covered, they set, check for blitzes, and if none, look to their outside and help where needed.

Just as in their regular drop protection, the tackles block on, or outside, in the same manner.

The two deep backs check first for blitzes or hard-coming ends before releasing. If the defense is even, both backs step up with the inside foot and prepare to take on any shooters. If no backer is coming, they quickly look outside and block the first rusher showing outside their tackles. However, if the defense is odd, they still step up as before, but now immediately look outside for the first defender showing outside their tackles. Both backs, if no backer—or no end man—is rushing, take their assigned routes.

Finally, the slot back—having been alerted by the code signifying alternate blocking—clears the line of scrimmage and immediately turns in over the middle area at a depth of no more than four yards. He is an outlet for the quarterback, who may, if he chooses, release the ball in the vacated area.

9

Screens, Draws, Shovel, and Statue

Obvious passing situations are apparent to the defensive team. They are ready to surge forward with a strong, all-out rush to get to the quarterback and prevent, or hurry, the throw.

THREE ROSE SCREENS

It is possible for the offensive team to use that rush to its own advantage. Hard-charging defensive linemen are sometimes suscep-tible to plays that first show pass and then end in the run. When these types of plays are successful, that defensive line tends to become wary and some of the heat is taken off the passer. The Tight-Slot attack uses screens, draws, a shovel pass, and a statue to slow down that defensive charge. There are three screens, slot-side, off-side, and middle (Figures 9-1, 9-2, 9-3).

Position Play

In the slot-side and off-side screens, the three quick receivers streak upfield exactly as though running a pass route. After the pass, they become blockers.

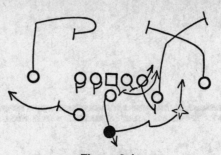

Figure 9-1
Rose Slot-Side Screen

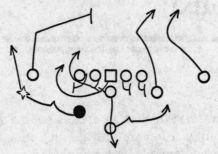

Figure 9-2
Rose Off-Side Screen

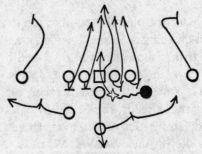

Figure 9-3
Rose Middle Screen

The interior linemen set and hit as in drop-back pass protection. Then the center and pulling guard release, get to the flank
and turn upfield as lead blockers.

Both deep backs set, bump, and roll outside. The quarterback drops, quick sets, drops again, and releases.

Coaching Points

It is most important that the timing of the play be correct. To insure proper timing, the center and pulling guard think, "Set-and-set-and-go." On the "go" they sprint to the flank and then turn upfield to give interference for the ball carrier. In taking their path to the corner, they must pass in front of their tackle and stay behind the line of scrimmage. By the same token, both deep backs must use the same court, in the same rhythm, before swinging to the outside. So must the quarterback. In addition, the quarterback must look upfield all the time he is in retreat. He must not look at the actual receiver until he is ready to release the ball. That ball is delivered on the "go." Only with unified actions by all can we get the correct timing for the screen. If the pulling linemen pull to the flank too soon, it is a dead giveaway to the defense who will immediately read screen and recover to stop the play. We are convincing them that the play is, indeed, a pass. And, we want the defensive backs, especially the linebackers, to quickly take their regular drops away from the line of scrimmage. That will give us running room after the ball has been caught.

Position Play

As before, both ends sprint upfield and give every indication of pass. All interior linemen set and repeat to themselves exactly as in the previous screens. On the "go" they release upfield and, closing together, form a running wedge for the ball carrier. Both the deep back and the quarterback go through their same routine, but the slot back, staying low and hidden, slides on the "go" to a spot behind his center. There he catches the ball and follows the wedge upfield.

Coaching Points

Again, timing is of paramount importance. All must act in unison. As before, we are convincing the defense that a pass is in progress. We want those backers and deep defenders to be moving away from the line of scrimmage, and as in the two previous screens, the quarterback must keep his eyes looking upfield until the instant he is ready to lob the ball to the slot back. In so doing, he must have to jump to get the ball over the hands of the rushers, but that is no great problem.

ROSE 34–DRAW AND 46–DRAW

Another method used to discourage the all-out rush is the draw play. The Tight-Slot uses two draw plays and opens the hole with regular 4 or 6 trap blocking (Figures 9-4, 9-5).

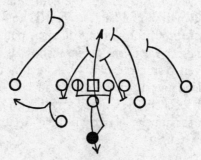

Figure 9-4
Rose 34-Draw: Block 4

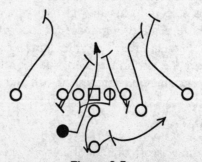

Figure 9-5
Rose 46-Draw: Block 6

Position Play

In both 34 and 46 draws, the entire line and slot back do exactly as described in their regular base blocking rules, there is one important exception: both tackles pass set briefly before taking their approach to block the linebackers.

Both deep backs set, and the designated ball carrier must not move forward until after the ball has been placed in his pocket. Only then does he drive into the hole.

The quarterback takes his normal drop-back course and slips the ball to the planned runner as he goes by. He then sets and fakes a throw.

Coaching Points

Just like the screens, these draw plays must be correctly timed. We cannot let the tackles move across the line of scrimmage at once as in a 4 or 6 running play. Again, we want those backers going away, so the tackles, at the snap of the ball, think, "set-and-go" and do just that. They set for one count and then go. Both deep backs cannot straighten up. They must remain as low as their original stance. In so doing they are, to some extent, hidden from the charging defensive line and can often get into the hit area before those defenders are aware of what is happening. Because these plays are relatively quick, the slot back and ends can block at once as they reach their downfield opponents. Finally, after slipping the ball off, the quarterback completes his drop and fakes throwing.

ROSE 26-SHOVEL PASS

The last two plays in this group differ in their approach and lend an element of surprise beyond the usual screens and draws. The first of these is Rose 26-Shovel Pass. This play takes the ball deep away from the line of scrimmage and then tosses it close to the slot back who carries it forward behind 6-trap blocking (Figure 9-6).

Both ends sprint upfield as though getting ready to catch the ball. They block when they reach the deep defenders.

The interior line executes regular 6 trap blocking, but once

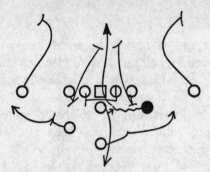

Figure 9-6
Rose 26-Shovel Pass: Block 6

again the tackles delay as before in taking their approach to the line backers.

Both deep backs act as they do on our screen plays. The quarterback makes his usual drop and then makes an underhanded toss to the slot back who has slipped into the middle area behind his center.

Coaching Points

Once more we have a timing consideration. Just as in our draw plays, the tackles must think and act "set-and-go" before going forward to block the linebackers. As always, we want those people to take their regular drops. The slot back must think the same "set-and-go" before he starts to his spot behind the center. He must stay low. As in the draws, he, too, may be hidden enough to remain undetected until too late. The quarterback, after making his toss, must get both hands in his ear and look upfield as though getting ready to pass. The immediate downfield blockers do not hesitate. The play is quick enough for getting into the line of scrimmage before they have reached the deep secondary.

ROSE 40–STATUE

Our final play is Rose 40-Statue. This is another feinted pass that ends as a sweep to the slot side. We are pulling in the corner defender and then running around him (Figure 9-7).

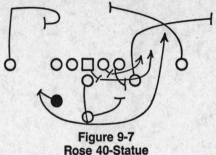

Figure 9-7
Rose 40-Statue

Position Play

Each player acts exactly as he did in our slot-side screen—with two exceptions. The fullback knocks the crashing end defender down, or gets him inside, as he makes his determined rush at our quarterback. The halfback sets, spins around, and takes the ball from the handoff by the quarterback. Then he sprints around the end behind his pulling guard and center.

Coaching Points

Of course this is another delay play. The center and pulling guard must think exactly as they did in our screens and so must the halfback. "Set-and-set-and-go" is the byword! The halfback cannot start too soon because that would be a dead giveaway. We want that crashing end on our slot side coming in hard to get at our quarterback. The fullback must not go to meet that end. We want that end in close when the ball is handed to our running back. That being so, we have a great deal of room permitting the ball carrier to sweep around him and pick up his blockers. The quarterback must hold the ball at shoulder height as he makes his drop. Then when he reaches the exchange area, he plants his outside foot, makes a half turn to face the halfback, and slips him the ball.

10

Audibles for the
Tight-Slot Attack

TAKE ADVANTAGE OF
DEFENSIVE ALIGNMENTS

From time to time certain defenses present the attacking team with an opportunity for substantial gain that is not usually present. Very often these misalignments result from faulty spacing in the defensive line, linebackers, and deep secondary posture. In addition, individual actions by certain members of the defense can also be exploited. Many times these indicators do not become apparent until the offense is out of the huddle and ready to go. However, the quarterback can impart a desired change in play by the use of an audible. When the quarterback wishes to audible, he first indicates his change in plan by calling out the snap number given in the huddle and then the number of the new play. This call is made twice to avoid confusion and to allow for the necessary mental adjustment. For example, if play 41 had been called in the huddle with the snap count on the second "hit," the quarterback changes the play on the line of scrimmage by calling out, "2-34; 2-34." Now the team is alerted that the original play has been cancelled, and

that play 34 will be run in its place. However, if the quarterback
wishes to give a false call at the time, he might cry, "1-34; 1-34."
Because the snap count was on the second "hit," the new call is
meaningless.

34–TRAP

The first play in the group used for audibles is 34-Trap. It can
be run from any formation, and is best utilized when we are pre-
sented with an even defense in which the defensive guards are too
far apart (Figure 10-1).

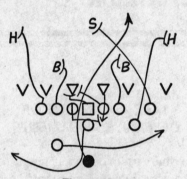

Figure 10-1
34-Trap Versus Wide Guards

Position Play

The entire front wall, end to end, execute their base 4 block
rule. The quarterback reverses out, hands to the fullback, and, in
this case, usually rolls.

Coaching Points

This is one of the quickest plays in football. To ensure that it
gets underway without hesitation, it is important that there be no
contact of any kind between the fullback and quarterback—both of
whom are moving at top speed. Accordingly, the fullback aims his
run at the off guard, and the quarterback reverses in favor of the slot

side. There is no time for anything but getting the ball to the runner, so as soon as the quarterback gets the ball, he falls back with no attempt at any fake. As soon as the fullback feels the ball, he curves his course back toward, and then over, the original position of his center. Now, with the pulling off guard and the more or less erect position of the quarterback, the low-running fullback will be screened and will often pop from behind the block of the guard and be running free in the secondary before they are aware of his presence. If the downfield blockers do a good job, the fullback is going to go a long way.

20–DEEP REVERSE

Sometimes we find that the defensive end man on our off side comes in very hard and tight against our blockers when we run our inside reverse. Our 20-Deep Reverse takes advantage of that type of play (Figure 10-2).

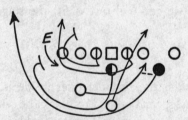

Figure 10-2
20-Deep Reverse Versus Tight Crashing End

Position Play

This deep reverse is blocked exactly like our 29-Reverse with one exception: the off guard who normally blocks out at the corner, now fakes that block, slips inside, and becomes a lead blocker.

Coaching Points

It is very important that the quarterback not give his interest away by rushing to the corner. Just the opposite. After he hands off to the halfback, he continues a deliberate roll. There is no hurry because the play does not develop that quickly. He runs, almost nonchalantly, to a spot outside, but parallel to, that hard-charging defender. He then stops and faces inside. His vision is now focused on that defender and it is a simple matter to handle him. If that player tries to recover with depth, the quarterback gets his head and shoulders across him, applies a cross-body block, and maintains a high bridge. Should that defender try to recover to the outside, he must go through the spot where the quarterback is ready and waiting. Now, a high shoulder block will eliminate him from the play.

40-JET

Some teams, when our flow is to the slot-side, have sent the off-end defender in hard and fast pursuit of the play. He is taking off fast and inside at the snap of the ball and his eyes and attention are concerned with that snap. If that style of play becomes relatively constant so that we can feel sure of it, the stage is set for 40-Jet (Figures 10-3, 10-4).

Position Play

The off end, if the first defender inside is close, slams that defender and then sprints upfield to block the wide deep defender.

If a defender is on him, the off tackle blocks that man. If no defender covers him, the tackle will block the linebacker. The off guard applies the same rule.

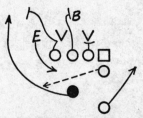

Figure 10-3
40-Jet Versus Even Defense

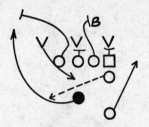

Figure 10-4
40-Jet Versus Odd Defense

The halfback, first gaining a little depth, sprints wide and is prepared to catch the ball at once.

Stepping out with his near foot, the quarterback zips an underhanded toss to his halfback.

All the players on the slot side sift through the line of scrimmage, sprint to the running lane, and block downfield.

Coaching Points

This is a very fast pitch and the halfback must get away with full speed. He must also be aware that the ball is coming to him very quickly and with pace. This is not a toss play. Accordingly, the quarterback must put some zip on the ball. He can best do that by lowering his back knee as he makes his throw. That gives the ball a rising trajectory and so makes it an easier catch for the halfback.

SUCKER PLAY

Because we pull our guard a great deal to block at the corner, lead or trap, some defending guards, or backers, come across very fast to try to catch the runner while he is still behind the line of scrimmage. We use two different types of play to counter and discourage that move. The first of these is very simple. We simply call it "sucker play," because it takes advantage of an overeager defender, the "sucker," who is deserting his territory too soon (Figures 10-5, 10-6).

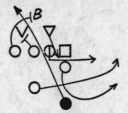

Figure 10-5
Sucker Play Versus Even Defense

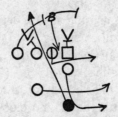

Figure 10-6
Sucker Play Versus Odd Defense

Position Play

The off guard pulls to the slot side and blocks the first man he meets. The off tackle blocks on; outside—as does the center. The off end blocks the first backer, his side. Reversing out, the quarterback slips the ball to the fullback who is driving into the area vacated by the crashing defender. As in jet blocking, all the slotside linemen filter through the line of scrimmage and block downfield.

Coaching Points

Here we have no great complications. We just want to get that fullback in there fast to take advantage of the hole opened by the actions of the defense.

45–DELAY

The second method used to handle those fast-pursuing defenders is called 45-Delay. Here we trap the off-side defensive

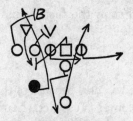

Figure 10-7
45-Delay Versus Even Defense

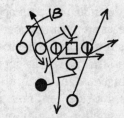

Figure 10-8
45-Delay Versus Odd Defense

tackle after our guards have pulled to the slot side. The ball is tossed
to our halfback on a delayed hit (Figures 10-7, 10-8).

Position Play

Both guards are pulling to the slot side and will block the first
defender they encounter. The rest of the slot-side linemen and the
slot back are hurrying downfield to block.

The off tackle blocks the first man to his inside and must get
his head across, and in front of, that defender. The off end slams
the first opponent inside and releases to block the linebacker on his
side.

The fullback drives into the area left by the pulling slot guard
and blocks anyone he meets.

The quarterback spins, recovers and slips the ball to his running back. Remaining low, that back has taken one full step to the
slot side. He now pivots on that foot and drives into the hole.

That hole is opened by the center, who, first letting the off

guard clear, pulls and traps the first defender on, or beyond, the
position of his off tackle.

Coaching Points

This play is called a delay because of the actions of the center
and halfback. If the center is covered, he must step into that defender with his slot-side foot. That allows the guard to clear and
also lets the off-side tackle reach him in making his down block.
Now the center, using that foot as a brace, makes a quarter turn to
the off side, locates the defender and then applies an out block with
his back shoulder. The center, throughout his entire maneuver,
must keep low and, when making his approach to his block, must
run an inside-out curve so that he will be approaching that defender
from the most advantageous angle. And the ball carrier, the
halfback, in making his slot-side step, must make a complete body
turn so that he faces the sideline. In addition, he must stay low and
hidden. The quarterback spins out, jerks his shoulders toward the
fullback to aid in the deception, and then steps toward the off side.
That step is parallel to the line of scrimmage.

40–TEAR SWEEP

We have been, from time to time, suddenly confronted by a
Gap-8 defensive alignment. When that happens, we like to check
our play and audible to 40-Tear Sweep (Figure 10-9).

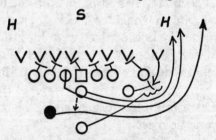

Figure 10-9
40-Tear Sweep Versus Gap-8 Defense

Position Play

The slot-side linemen and the center all block away from the slot. The slot back blocks the end man in the defensive front. All the off-side players, except the off guard, fill inside. The off guard is a lead blocker. The fullback, if needed, helps with the defensive end man or blocks downfield. The quarterback reverses, tosses to the running back, and leads. The halfback secures the ball and sprints around the corner.

Coaching Points

The important thing here is to get the end defender out of the way and run at the corner with all possible speed—we "tear" at that corner. All of the on-line blockers must be certain to get their heads across the crotches of the defenders to prevent any penetration.

93–LOOK IN AND 97–LOOK IN

The remaining group of plays covers passes that take advantage of varied defensive secondary postures. The first of these is 93-Look In and is used against a too close, or no, backer on the slot side. Next is 97-Look In, which is utilized when the same conditions apply on the off side (Figures 10-10, 10-11).

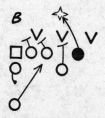

Figure 10-10
93-Look In Versus Inside Backer

Figure 10-11
97-Look In Versus Close Backer

Position Play

All covered linemen fire out at the knees of the defenders across from them. All uncovered linemen block at the knees of the on-line defender closest to them and our center. The fullback drives hard over his guard on the play side. The play-side end, expecting the pass immediately, releases on a slight inside angle to catch the ball. The quarterback takes the ball from the center, straightens up, jumps vertically, and flips the ball to his receiver.

Coaching Points

The blocking linemen must block at the defenders' knees. That brings their hands down and away from the flight path of the ball. The fullback must drive fast and hard to hold that backer in position. That, of course, clears the reception area for the end, and that end must not be more than four yards in depth. Otherwise, he will be too close to the deep defenders. Finally, the quarterback cannot delay. He seizes the ball, straightens, and in the same movement, leaps straight up, holding the ball high. Now a simple flick of his wrist is all that is needed to get the ball to his end.

90–ALLEY PASS

Last, we come to 90-Alley Pass. From time to time, defending teams, in an attempt to shut off our running game, present us with a 9-man front. This can be a 5-4-2, or a 6-3-2, and both are excellent

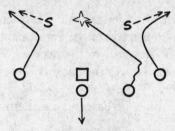

Figure 10-12
90-Alley Pass Versus 2-Deep Defense

against the run, however they are both weak against the alley pass, which has but two deep defenders (Figure 10-12).

Position Play

Alley Pass uses regular, or alternate, pass protection. Both ends drive at the outside shoulders of the deep defenders, and then break at a 45-degree angle toward the flag. The slot back starts slowly at a slight outside angle, and then breaks to the relatively deep middle and prepares to receive the throw.

Coaching Points

It is essential that the slot back not arrive in the catch area too soon. He allows just enough time for the two deep defenders to get into pursuit of his ends, and they must pursue. In no way can they ignore them. Of course, they are now becoming widely separated, and the middle area is deserted. This is a no-win situation for the two deep defenders; no matter what they do, they cannot possibly cover three deep receivers—one is bound to be open.

CHECK TO ALTERNATE PROTECTION

There can be times during the game that our quarterback might wish to change from regular to alternate pass protection after the team has reached the line of scrimmage and is set in Rose or Liz. He does this by simply calling out a code word, and that word is any word beginning with the letter "A." He then repeats the play number and the team is ready to go. For example, our quarterback has directed Rose 72-Pass on 2 in the huddle. When the team is at the line of scrimmage, he sees the backers very close and suspects a blitz. He cries out, "Able-Able-2-72-2-72." Now the team is alerted that we will throw 72-Pass and use alternate pass protection.

11

Basic Tight-Slot Drills

WHY DRILLS?

In putting together the Tight-Slot attack, a good deal of attention is paid to group and individual drills. A team's ability to rise to the occasion depends to a very great extent on drills. Meaningful, well-planned drills tend to assure success in the game. The importance of these drills cannot be overestimated. Wherever possible, it is good to let the players assist in teaching each other, while the coach stands by and lends help when and where needed. This player involvement not only keeps interest high, but actually helps them to learn more about what they are doing. An alert, intelligent player has a great advantage.

BASIC TIGHT-SLOT DRILLS

Because the Tight-Slot places emphasis on the running game, a great deal of work is done on correct blocking techniques. In the early stages, most of the work is done on an individual basis. Following this, most of the teaching is done in group drills.

STANCE DRILL

To block effectively, the blocker must begin with a good stance. Our stance allows for a quick, powerful movement forward and, at the same time, permits the blocker to pull out of the line to trap or lead.

We have the players place their feet at about shoulder width with a foot-to-foot relationship of no more than back toe to forward instep. The down hand is placed just inside the back knee and is perpendicular to the ground. The other arm is folded over the thigh of the front leg. Back, neck and head are parallel to the ground, and weight is evenly distributed over the feet and down hand.

To drill for stance, players are lined up in a front. At the command "Set," they assume the correct stance and the coach goes down the line checking each player. As the players progress, they are paired and, with only needed help from the coach, run the drill themselves (Figure 11-1).

Ô Ô Ô Ô Ô

Figure 11-1
Drill for Stance

SHOULDER BLOCK

The shoulder block is the basis of all blocking, and a great deal of effort is made to perfect its technique. We start by showing the players how to use their heads and shoulders. The blocker assumes a kneeling position on both knees and close to a standing dummy held by a teammate. He then places his face mask in the middle of the dummy and slides his cheek alongside. This brings his shoulder in contact with the dummy. The same side arm—flexed at the elbow—is extended to increase the blocking surface. He bulls his neck and looks up. In this position, the blocker is able to pinch the defender with his neck and extended arm-shoulder, and so able to control his lateral movement. This drill teaches the correct position for the head, neck, and shoulder. This form is practiced with the head on alternate sides of the dummy.

The next step is to teach the blocker to block with force. The dummy is moved away a short distance and the player fires out now aided by the swing of the arm of the blocking shoulder. The blocker must deliver the blow forward—not up. This movement is practiced on the two-man blocking sled. Here, again players are encouraged to assist each other (Figure 11-2).

Figure 11-2
Hitting Out on Two-Man Sled

This hitting drill is next, followed by teaching the player to step forward with either foot and simultaneously strike a blow with the shoulder on the same side as the advancing foot. With the use of leg-arm movement, the blocker applies his thrust. He must aim directly at the middle of his opponent so as not to tip off his intent by immediately placing his face to one side or the other. It is just before contact that he slips his head to the desired side. As soon as contact is made, vigorous leg drive provides the follow-through. The blocker must think in terms of blocking beyond his opponent. As his legs continue their drive, the blocker works his hips into the hole. The defender is driven first back, and then laterally. Players vie with each other to see who can hit with the most force.

THE CHUTE DRILL

To further develop offensive blocking, a great deal of work is done in the chute. This drill places the five interior linemen in individual tunnels. In each tunnel a 2 × 7 plank, 6 feet long, is placed. A standing dummy is placed on each plank and held by a player. The blockers line up at the head of the chute, and on the count, fire out into the dummy and proceed to drive it down the length of the plank against the resistance of the holder. The chute keeps the blockers from rising, the plank keeps their feet from

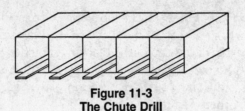

Figure 11-3
The Chute Drill

closing together, and the resistance builds strength. It is also an excellent device for getting the linemen off in unison (Figure 11-3).

REVERSE SHOULDER BLOCK

Because a great many of our assignments call for blocking down, every effort is made to perfect the reverse shoulder block. The teaching is exactly the same as that used in teaching the regular shoulder block—with this exception. In applying the reverse shoulder block, the blocker takes a short step in the direction of his opponent and parallel to the line of scrimmage. The blocker's helmet is thrust across the defender's crotch, and the blocker hits with the shoulder opposite this stepping foot. As soon as he makes contact, the blocker follows through with short, choppy steps and drives his opponent down the line of scrimmage. Two things are accomplished with this: first, the defender is kept from crossing the line of scrimmage, and second, the hole is widened as he is driven in a lateral direction. That increases the room for running (Figure 11-4).

Figure 11-4
The Reverse Shoulder Block

TRAP BLOCK

This technique is used to block out at the corners, and in interior trap plays. It is most important that the approach to the

Figure 11-5
Trap at the Corner with Inside-Out Approach

Figure 11-6
Interior Trap with Inside-Out Approach

opponent be done correctly. It must be an "inside-out" curve, which enables the blocker to get an inside angle and stronger thrust through the defender (Figures 11-5, 11-6).

The same technique is used in the interior trapping game, only the approach is much shorter.

LEVERAGE DRILL

In this drill, we are training the linemen to get good leverage in their blocking. Setting up in their regular stance, they alternate quick charges with attention focused on dipping under the defender's hands and lifting with the shoulders (Figure 11-7).

Figure 11-7
Leverage Drill

CROSS-BODY BLOCK

Here we teach the fundamentals of the cross-body block. Players are paired and they alternate holding a standing dummy. Using his right side, the blocker shoots his right hand high across the bag, hits the bag with his right hip and, using a crab-like move, drives against the bag. If hitting with his left side, the procedure is reversed (Figure 11-8).

Figure 11-8
Drill for Cross-Body Block

RUNNING SHOULDER BLOCK

In teaching this block, we stress the same fundamentals as in the normal block, but now the approach is on the run. We begin with the blocker at a walk. Just before striking the dummy, he gives a head fake to the side opposite his hitting shoulder, and then applies the block itself. He must keep his feet well apart for balance and his back straight. As the drill progresses, the blocker moves at a trot and, finally, at a run. The last step discards the dummy, and the blocker works against a live player (Figure 11-9).

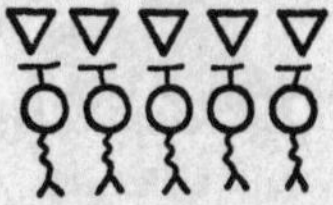

Figure 11-9
Running Shoulder Block

RUNNING CROSS-BODY BLOCK

Once again, the same techniques are taught, but with the blocker on the move. He begins at a walk, moves to a trot, and finally runs. After the dummy has been removed and the blocker is working against a teammate, that player is instructed to catch the blocker after the hit (Figure 11-10).

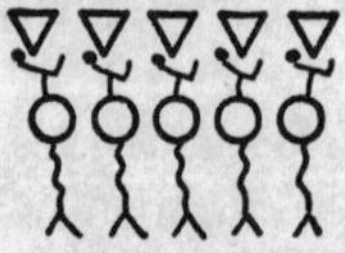

Figure 11-10
Running Cross-Body Block

12

Drills for the Running Game

Through the use of group drills, the players receive concentrated individual attention. Here they see a variety of defenses and alignments and comprehend how to handle them. The players are shown how they can help each other when faced with the unusual. It is that awareness which is the mark of a well-drilled team. The Tight-Slot attack has a number of drills—lettered for convenience—that duplicate what actually happens in a game, and portray a wide selection of situations. The first of these is the "A" Drill (Figures 12-1 through 12-12).

"A" DRILL: INSIDE ATTACK

Coaching Points

Always checking stance and takeoff, we are particularly interested in correct techniques. Is the cross blocking guard stepping out at a 45-degree angle to allow the tackle to clear? Is he keeping his low position and not raising? Does the tackle get his head across

Figure 12-1
3-Block Versus Even Defense

Figure 12-2
3-Block Versus Odd Defense

Figure 12-3
3-Block Versus Gap Defense

the defender's crotch and prevent penetration? Are the blockers assigned to the linebackers taking the correct approach angle? Are they hitting in the numbers and screening vision? This is where all the mistakes must be corrected and automatic, proper reflexes developed.

Coaching Points

Still observing stance and takeoff, we now look especially at the blocking technique of the trapping guard. Is he taking an exact 45-degree pull so that he can see the defender and be in position to effectively block him? What does he do if the defender does not come across? Is he staying low? How about the center? Is he using the correct techniques? Against even defenses is he using a reverse shoulder block? Are the tackles blocking the backers in their numbers? Are we moving fast enough? Suppose the defender comes in so low we cannot hit him with the shoulder? Do we drop, smother, and roll him away with our thighs and knees?

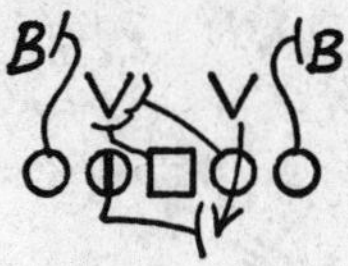

Figure 12-4
4-Block Versus Even Defense

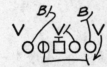

Figure 12-5
4-Block Versus Odd Defense

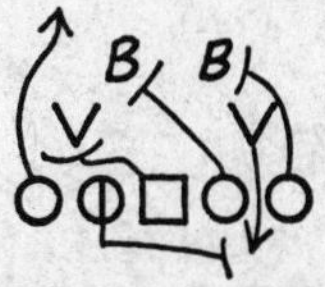

Figure 12-6
4-Block Versus Gap Defense

Coaching Points

The 6-Block is exactly like the 4-Block in all its techniques. We look for the same things here as in blocking 4-Trap.

Figure 12-7
6-Block Versus Even Defense

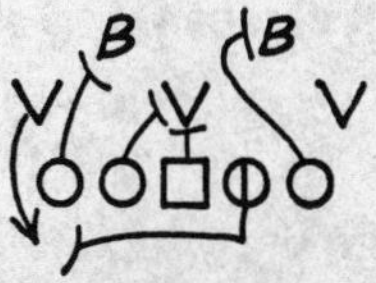

Figure 12-8
6-Block Versus Odd Defense

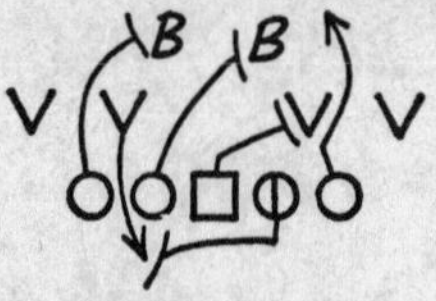

Figure 12-9
6-Block Versus Gap Defense

Coaching Points

Here we are looking for a good block by the uncovered center. He must arrive ahead of the ball carrier.

Figure 12-10
7-Block Versus Even Defense

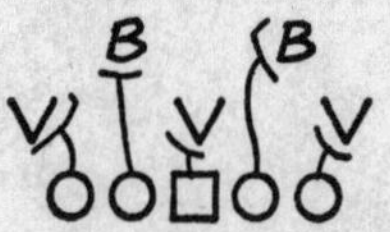

Figure 12-11
7-Block Versus Odd Defense

Figure 12-12
7-Block Versus Gap Defense

The next is the "B" group, which is concerned with the attack at the corner (Figures 12-13 through 12-24).

"B" DRILL: CORNER ATTACK

Coaching Points

Constantly checking stance and start, we look to see if the slot back is executing correctly. Is he first stepping forward with his inside foot to allow the slot end to cross? Is he deliberate enough so that he does not immediately show the defensive end that he is about to block him? From his stance his step must come out low and he must block on the far leg of that end. If his initial thrust does not get that opponent down, he must crab and prevent him from skating outside. Look at the lead guard. Is he turning upfield close enough to the inside to prevent a seam that a defender might sift through? How about the off guard? Is his pull a deep enough arc to get him headed straight upfield as he goes upfield to lead? What

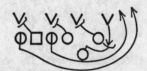

Figure 12-13
0-Block Versus Even Defense

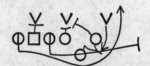

Figure 12-14
0-Block Versus Odd Defense

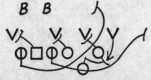

Figure 12-15
0-Block Versus Gap Defense

about the tackle and center? Are they using the corner techniques to prevent penetration and pursuit?

Coaching Points

Is the slot back staying low and stepping up as the slot end crosses? Does he seal the hole close enough to cut off the inside pursuit? Is the slot guard using the correct inside-out course as he approaches the corner? Is he driving his shoulder through the defender's numbers? Is the off guard coming fast enough? Will he get upfield with his shoulders parallel to the line so that he is prepared to block to either side?

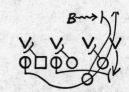

Figure 12-16
1-Block Versus Even Defense

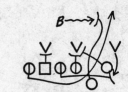

Figure 12-17
1-Block Versus Odd Defense

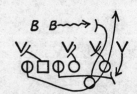

Figure 12-18
1-Block Versus Gap Defense

Coaching Points

Primarily we are looking at the blocks of the off end and tackle. Is the off end getting his head across the crotch of his opponent to prevent penetration? Is the tackle getting enough drive to open the area? Is he getting a good inside-out approach? Are his feet well spaced for balance as he makes contact?

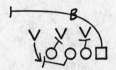

Figure 12-19
8X-Block Versus Even Defense

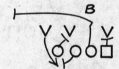

Figure 12-20
8X-Block Versus Odd Defense

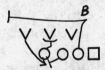

Figure 12-21
8X-Block Versus Gap Defense

Coaching Points

It is very important to check carefully the influence block by the off tackle. Does this, at the start, look exactly like his 8 X-Block? Is he slipping clean inside to get at his downfield block? Does he hit high enough to screen the vision of the end defender? How about the off end? Is he getting his head across the crotch of

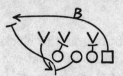

Figure 12-22
39-Pitch Block Versus Even Defense

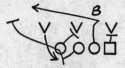

Figure 12-23
39-Pitch Block Versus Odd Defense

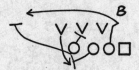

Figure 12-24
39-Pitch Block Versus Gap Defense

the defender and preventing penetration? Above all, the tackle must convince that end man so that defender will be fighting hard inside as the ball is being pitched outside.

"C" DRILL: 45–DELAY

Coaching Points

The big job here is to get coordination between the pull of the off guard to the slot side and the pull of the center to the off side. The center can't leave too quickly or he will be knocked off by the guard; and, if too late, will not find his target. Is the center taking a firm jab step forward with his slot-side foot? Never the other foot or he will fall over his own feet in trying to get back to his block. Does he step-delay-and then pull? Is he staying low to get into his inside-out approach to his block?

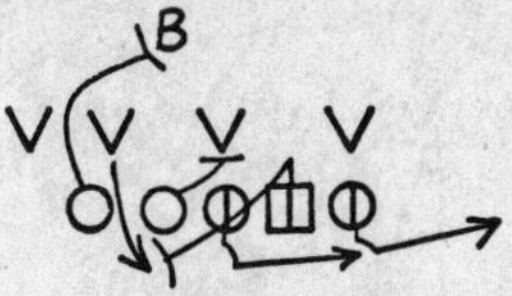

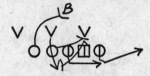

Figure 12-25
45-Delay Versus Even Defense

Figure 12-26
45-Delay Versus Odd Defense

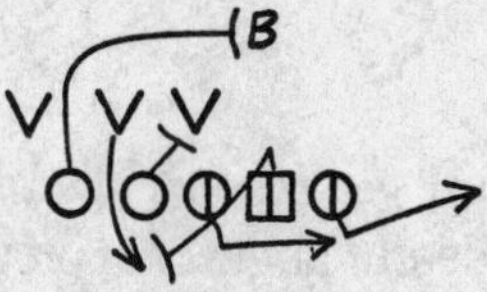

Figure 12-27
45-Delay Versus Gap Defense

ALTERNATE BLOCKING: INSIDE AND CORNER

Coaching Points

We must get the slot back through the hole ahead of the ball carrier. Accordingly, he is "cheated" a little deeper and a little inside. This will not be apparent to the defenders, and will insure that the slot back gets the job done.

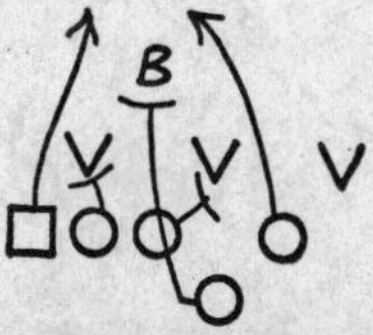

Figure 12-28
3-Block Versus Even Defense

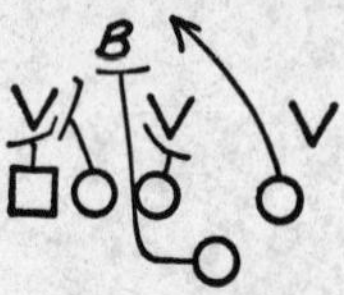

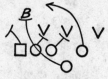

Figure 12-29
3-Block Versus Odd Defense

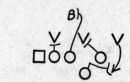

Figure 12-30
3-Block Versus Gap Defense

Coaching Points

The slot back must get a good block. Is he jab-stepping forward to get a good inside-out angle of approach? Is he staying low to get good leverage at contact? Is he deliberate enough in his first move to give that defender time to get some depth? How about the end? Is he getting his head across the crotch of his man to prevent penetration?

Figure 12-31
1-Block Versus Even Defense

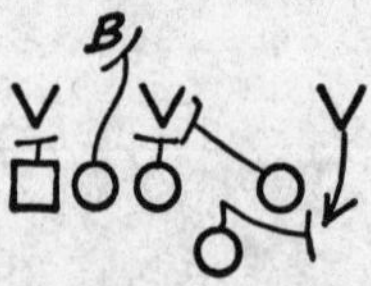

Figure 12-32
1-Block Versus Odd Defense

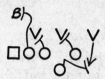

Figure 12-33
1-Block Versus Gap Defense

Coaching Points

The essential point here is to get the off tackle to run a good inside-out approach. Are his feet well spread to maintain balance? Is he low enough to hit with good force? How about the blocks on the backers? Is the angle of approach correct? Are the blockers screening the vision of the backers? Are the remaining linemen preventing penetration?

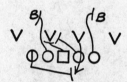

Figure 12-34
4-Trap Block Versus Even Defense

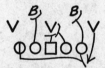

Figure 12-35
4-Trap Block Versus Odd Defense

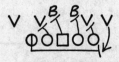

Figure 12-36
4-Trap Block Versus Gap Defense

Coaching Points

What we are looking for here is the correct execution of the cross block by our guard and tackle. Is the tackle getting across fast enough and is his head getting across the crotch of his man to prevent penetration? Is the guard getting an inside-out approach to his target?

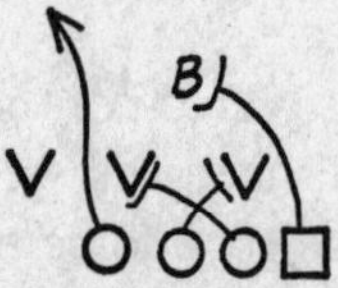

Figure 12-37
7-Drive Block Versus Even Defense

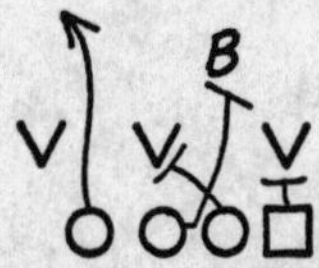

Figure 12-38
7-Drive Block Versus Odd Defense

Figure 12-39
7-Drive Block Versus Gap Defense

Coaching Points

Is the pulling guard getting a good inside-out angle of approach? Is he hitting high enough to screen the defender's vision? Is he convincing the defender that 8X is in progress? Is the remainder of the line preventing penetration?

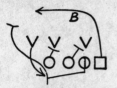

Figure 12-40
39-Pitch Block Versus Even Defense

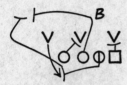

Figure 12-41
39-Pitch Block Versus Odd Defense

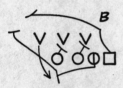

Figure 12-42
39-Pitch Block Versus Gap Defense

13

Drills for the Passing Game

Many coaches believe that the best defense against the pass is to rush the passer. To sack the passer before he can throw is the ultimate objective. However, if he can be made to hurry his throw, and so disrupt the timing of the play, that is also acceptable. Accordingly, defensive teams use various stratagems to gain either of these objectives.

"X" DRILL

To offset those schemes, the Tight-Slot uses the "X" drills to train pass protectors in defeating the most common of those plans. Only by constant repetition of these drills can the offense become proficient in handling those maneuvers successfully. That is the objective of the "X" drills (Figures 13-1 through 13-17).

PLAY-ACTION PROTECTION

Coaching Points

In checking the off side of the line -A- we want to see that the center does not allow any penetration. He is not required to move

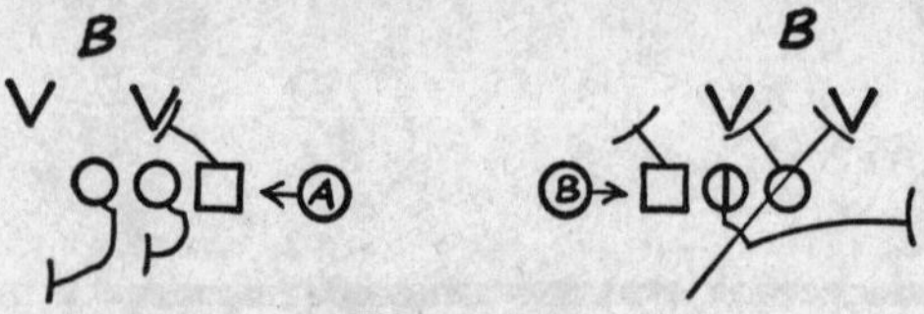

Figure 13-1
Play-Action Protection Versus Even Defense
Red or Blue

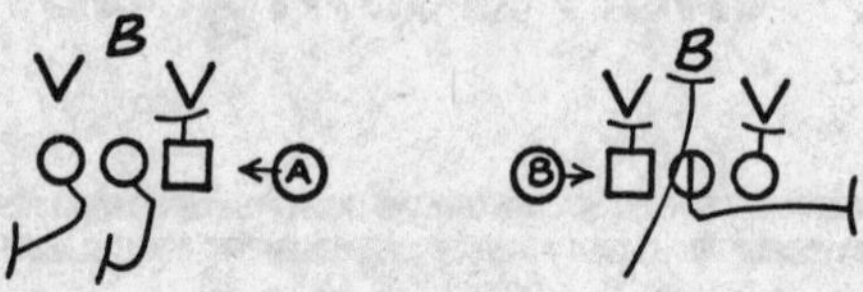

Figure 13-2
Play-Action Protection Versus Odd Defense
Red or Blue

an opponent, but he is expected to keep him from getting onto our line. Both guard and tackle, in making the hinge block, must do it correctly. Does it look like the first step in a pull? Are they keeping low? Do they then pivot in time to pick off the off-side chase?

In group -B- we want the tackle to keep the defender where he is. He does not have to move him. Does the pulling guard take an inside-out path to the corner? Finally, the fullback must hit the correct area. If the defense is even, he hits over the tackle space; and, if odd, over the area of his guard.

Coaching Points

The off-side blockers act exactly as they do in base blocking the 7 hole. If the center is covered, he will have the help of one of the guards; if uncovered, he will assist the guard who is playing the most dangerous opponent. The same conditions apply to the slot-side blockers. No uncovered lineman may set. He must block on the line of scrimmage. Only by making an aggressive block can he convince the opposition that a running play is in progress.

Figure 13-3
Play-Action Protection Versus Even Defense
White

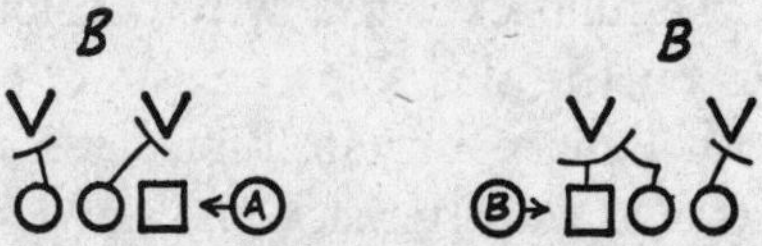

Figure 13-4
Play-Action Protection Versus Odd Defense
White

BASIC DROP-BACK PROTECTION

Coaching Points

Are the covered offensive players quick in setting up? Do they hit-retreat-and hit again? How about the uncovered men? Do they set quickly and always look from left to right to ascertain where they can lend assistance? Above all, no defender can be permitted to take an inside path to the ball!

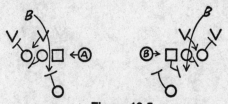

Figure 13-5
Basic Protection Versus Even Defense

Figure 13-6
Basic Protection Versus Odd Defense

BASIC PROTECTION VERSUS BLITZ

Coaching Points

Here we have an added dimension with a blitzing linebacker. It is very important to quickly pick up the off-side blitz because the quarterback can't see it as he drops back with his eyes turned away. In consequence, the fullback is totally responsible for that backer. Now, the backer on the slot side can get in rather easily. The uncovered center will make a try for him, but is not apt to be fully successful. However, the quarterback and slot back are keying that defender. No matter what the call, if that backer comes, the ball is dumped to the slot back as both he and the quarterback have reacted correctly to their key.

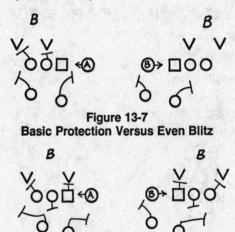

Figure 13-7
Basic Protection Versus Even Blitz

Figure 13-8
Basic Protection Versus Odd Blitz

BASIC PROTECTION VERSUS TWISTS

Coaching Points

In both -A- and -B-, the offensive tackles must stay with their assignment. Inside, over, outside the tackles are responsible for

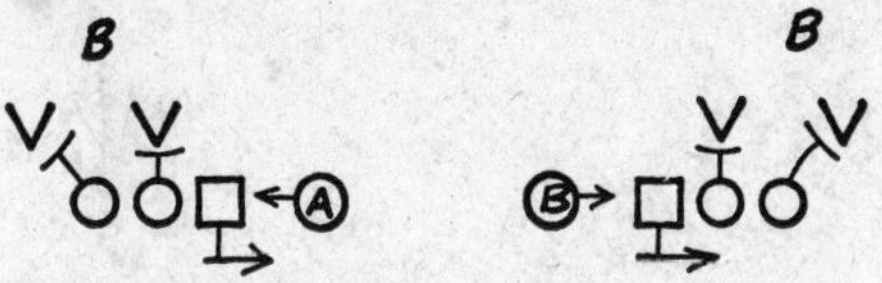

Figure 13-9
Basic Protection Versus Even Twist

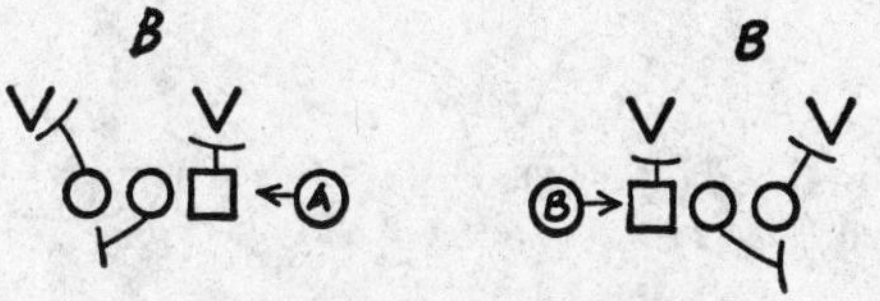

Figure 13-10
Basic Protection Versus Odd Twist

those defenders. Now the guards, if covered, also go with their assigned rushers. But, if they are uncovered, they set and look immediately outside to lend any help needed. Meanwhile, the fullback is still responsible for the off-side backer and the quarterback and slot back, together, key and defeat the slot-side backer.

ALTERNATE DROP-BACK PROTECTION

Coaching Points

In both -A- and -B-, the covered linemen set-hit, set-hit. They must never let the defender take an inside course to the quarterback. The uncovered linemen set and look for shooting backers. If those backers are coming they take them. This also applies to the halfback and fullback when the defense is even. Agaisnt an odd defense, they take the first rushers outside their tackles. In both cases they must first step up with the inside foot as they check their responsibilities.

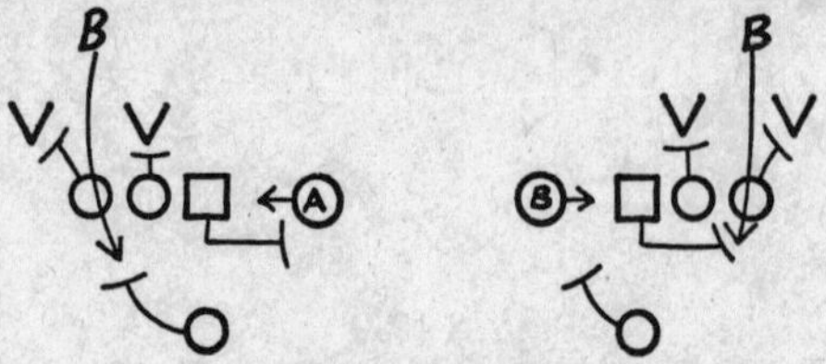

Figure 13-11
Alternate Protection Versus Even Defense

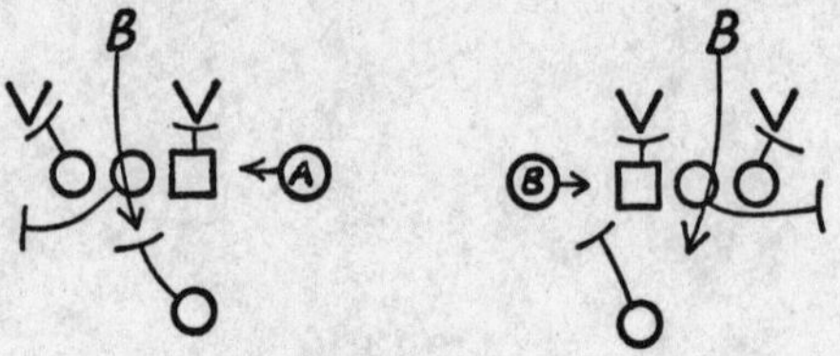

Figure 13-12
Alternate Protection Versus Odd Defense

ALTERNATE PROTECTION VERSUS BLITZ

Coaching Points

Here we see uncovered linemen playing as always: set-hit-set-hit- until the pass is thrown. However, the uncovered guards in an even defense are responsible for any shooting backers. In both odd and even, the deep backs divide. If the defense is even, they step up with the inside foot and check the backers. If one is blitzing, that back will stay with him. In the odd defense, the deep backs

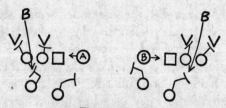

Figure 13-13
Alternate Protection Versus Even Blitz

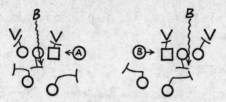

Figure 13-14
Alternate Protection Versus Odd Blitz

must again step up first, but now they are checking for the first defender outside.

ALTERNATE PROTECTION VERSUS TWISTS

Coaching points

The covered players must stay with their assigned opponents, no matter where they go. The deep backs are responsible for the backers on their respective sides. As they take a short step up with the inside foot, they are watching those backers. When they see them twisting behind their in-charging teammates, the deep backs

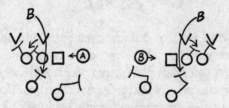

Figure 13-15
Alternate Protection Versus Even Twist

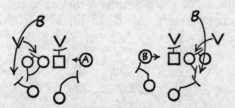

Figure 13-16
Alternate Protection Versus Odd Twist

are waiting to take them on. The deep backs are always responsible for backers first.

Coaching Points

This is most often seen in a 5-2 defense. The main thing here is that the uncovered guards, who are responsible for the blitzers and twisters, must be alert to the fact that when the backer in front of them is going away inside, it is very likely that the backer from that side may be coming. Accordingly, the guards regard away backers in a suspicious light, and so are prepared and looking for the backer coming from the other side.

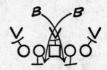

Figure 13-17
Alternate Protection Versus Double Twist

"Y" DRILL

Our "Y" drill is a skeletal arrangement made up of our backs and ends. Here we are looking to polish our passing attack. We always have pass defenders playing our receivers. Only in that way, we believe, can our passers and receivers coordinate correctly. Furthermore, our passers and receivers must read keys who are in that defensive backfield. We are first concerned with our play-action passes, and run all of them against a 3-deep and then a 4-deep defensive backfield (Figures 13-18, 13-19, 13-20, 13-21).

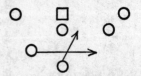

Figure 13-18
Red or Blue Versus 3-Deep

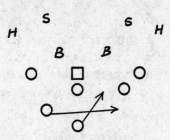

Figure 13-19
Red or Blue Versus 4-Deep

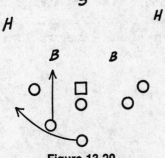

Figure 13-20
White Versus 3-Deep

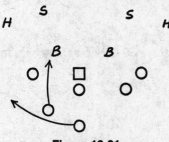

Figure 13-21
White Versus 4-Deep

Coaching Points

From these sets we run every play-action pass. We are first concerned that the receivers run their routes correctly. Then we look to the passer to get the ball away at the proper time. Most passers are inclined to hold the ball too long, which not only increases the chances of their being sacked, but also gives the defenders more time to recover to the receiver. Finally, they must correctly read, and react to, the keys they see in the defensive backfield.

"Z" DRILL

This is the same group that made up our "Y" drill. Here however, we are working on our drop-back passing game. We throw all our 60 series passes against defenses that are 3-deep, and our 70 series is used similarly against 4-deep coverages (Figures 13-22, 13-23).

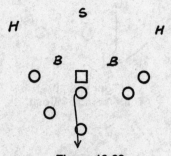

Figure 13-22
Rose 60 Series Versus 3-Deep

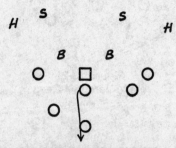

Figure 13-23
Rose 70 Series Versus 4-Deep

Coaching Points

In these drop-back passes, both 3-deep and 4-deep, we again deploy a defensive secondary to provide more game-like reality. Our receivers must get practice in running their routes correctly even when getting an occasional bump. Our passer must learn to release the ball just before—not after—his receiver is in the clear. That's not possible to learn if there are no defenders, and—very important—our quarterback must learn to correctly key the actions in the defensive secondary. This is particularly true when the 70 series is used against the 4-deep. Moreover, he must learn to pick the open receiver. There is no way he can get the ball to the prime receiver if he is not open. Then the quarterback must throw to the secondary target.

"S" DRILL

Finally we come to our "S" drill, which is exclusively concerned with screens, draws, a shovel, and a statue. We do not reduce the group to skeletal form here. There is too much integrated and interrelated timing between all segments of the team to allow for segregation; accordingly, we always rehearse the "S" drill exactly as depicted and described in Chapter 9. It is a team drill.

Index